"It's not hyperbole to say, 'It's about time.' While there are good books out there telling pastors how to preach Christ from all the Scriptures, there have been very few Bible studies for laypeople—especially for women— along these lines. Nancy Guthrie does an amazing job of helping us to fit the pieces of the biblical puzzle together, with Christ at the center."

> **Michael Horton,** J. Gresham Machen Professor of Systematic
> Theology and Apologetics, Westminster Seminary California;
> author, *Calvin on the Christian Life*

"I am thankful to God to be able to offer Nancy Guthrie's series Seeing Jesus in the Old Testament to the women of our church. For too long, studies have led us only to see what we are to do. Now we can see through the pages of this series what Jesus has done! With Nancy's help, the story of redemption jumps off the pages of the Old Testament, and the truths of the gospel are solidified in women's hearts and lives."

> **Jo Coltrain,** Director of Women's Ministry, First Evangelical
> Free Church, Wichita, Kansas

"Nancy takes us by the hand and the heart on an exegetical excursion to see Christ in the Old Testament. The beauty of Guthrie's writing is that you are certain she has met him there first."

> **Jean F. Larroux,** Senior Pastor, Southwood Presbyterian Church,
> PCA, Huntsville, Alabama

"There are many great Christian books but not many great Bible studies. Nancy is a master of getting the Word of God into the mouths, hearts, and lives of her students. I cannot wait to share this study with my people."

> **Donna Dobbs,** Christian Education Director, First Presbyterian
> Church, Jackson, Mississippi

The Word of the Lord

**Other books in the
Seeing Jesus in the Old Testament series:**

The Word of the Lord

Seeing Jesus in the Prophets

(A 10-Week Study)

nancy guthrie

:: CROSSWAY®

WHEATON, ILLINOIS

Trade paperback ISBN: 978-1-4335-3660-1
ePub ISBN: 978-1-4335-3663-2
PDF ISBN: 978-1-4335-3661-8
Mobipocket ISBN: 978-1-4335-3662-5

Library of Congress Cataloging-in-Publication Data

Guthrie, Nancy.
   The word of the Lord : seeing Jesus in the prophets / Nancy Guthrie.
      pages cm.— (Seeing Jesus in the Old Testament series)
      Includes bibliographical references.
      ISBN 978-1-4335-3660-1 (tp)
      1. Bible. Prophets—Textbooks. 2. Bible. Prophets—Criticism, interpretation, etc. 3. Jesus Christ—Biblical teaching. I. Title.
BS1506.G88   2014
224'.064—dc23   2013044994

Crossway is a publishing ministry of Good News Publishers.

VP   26   25   24   23   22
16   15   14   13   12   11   10

To my friends at Crossway who entrusted me with the privilege
of writing the Seeing Jesus in the Old Testament series.

To Al Fisher, who has guided so much solid Christian
publishing over a long career. I am so grateful for your
initial invitation to write for Crossway and all of your wise
guidance and gracious encouragement along the way.

To Lydia Brownback, who brings so much experience and
insight to every project she touches. You have not only been
a terrific editor—you have become my trusted friend.

To Jon Marshall, who has brought creativity and commitment
to the most agonizing part of the project—putting it on
video. Just thinking about you makes me smile.

And most of all to Amy Kruis, who has championed
this series from the get-go and over the long haul. Your
enthusiasm has encouraged me, your professionalism has
impressed me, and your friendship has blessed me.

Contents

Before We Get Started

A Note from Nancy

The Prophetic Books of the Old Testament are the books of the Bible I have understood the least and avoided the most. And maybe you can relate to that. The prophets have strange names and do some strange things and communicate in some strange ways. But I don't want to be a stranger to them anymore. Since the whole of Scripture is "breathed out by God and profitable for teaching, for reproof, for correction, and for training in righteousness, that the man of God may be complete, equipped for every good work" (2 Tim. 3:16–17), why would I want to say there is an entire section of it that I don't really need to know about? Because I want to know God, I want to hear everything he has to say to me, and perhaps you can relate to that too. In this study we're going to dive into these challenging books with the aim of emerging with a sense of not only what God, through these prophets, had to say to his people in their own day, but also what he has to say to you and me.

There are three essential parts to this study. The first is the personal time you will spend reading your Bible, seeking to strengthen your grip on its truths as you work your way through the questions provided in the Personal Bible Study section of each week's lesson. This will be the easiest part to skip, but nothing is more important than reading and studying God's Word, expecting that he will meet you as you do. Because we will cover large chunks of Scripture that I will not be able to read through and explain in the Teaching Chapters or videos, the foundational understanding you will gain through your time doing the Personal Bible Study is essential.

As you work on the Personal Bible Study, try not to become frustrated if you can't come up with an answer to every question or if you're not sure what the question is getting at. The goal of the questions is not necessarily to record all the "right" answers but to get you into the passage and thinking it through in a fresh way. Certainly some answers to your lingering questions will become clearer as you read the chapter or watch the video and as you discuss the passage with your group.

The second part of each lesson is the Teaching Chapter, in which I seek to explain and apply the passage we are studying. The content of the teaching chapters is the same in both the book and the video. If you are using the videos, you can go ahead and read the chapter as a preview, if you'd like, or simply sit back and watch the video. Or you may prefer to come back and read the chapter after watching the video to seal in what you've heard. It's up to you. You can also download an audio or video version of the teaching chapters at http://www.crossway.com.

At the end of each Teaching Chapter is a short piece called "Looking Forward," which will turn your attention to how what you've just studied in that particular prophetic book offers insight into what is yet to come when Christ returns. So much of what these prophets wrote about who Jesus is and what he would do was accomplished at least in part at his first coming. But there is also much in these books regarding who he will be and what he will do at his second coming. That's what we'll take a peak at in the Looking Forward section of the teaching chapters. The Looking Forward sections are not included in the video, so if you are relying on the video for the teaching, be sure to return to it in the book as part of your group discussion or on your own.

The third part of each week's lesson is the time you spend with your group sharing your lives together and discussing what you've learned and what you're still trying to understand and apply. A Discussion Guide is included at the end of each week's lesson. You may want to follow it exactly, working through each question as written. Or you may just want to use the guide as an idea starter for your discussion, choosing the questions that suit your group and discussing the key insights you gained through the personal bible study and teaching chapter.

Each aspect is important—laying the foundation, building on it, and sealing it in. We all have different learning styles, so one aspect of the study will likely have more impact on you than another, but all three together will help you to truly "own" the truths in this study so that they can become a part of you as you seek to know your covenant God in deeper ways.

I've put together the sections of this study in a way that offers flexibility for how you can use it and in how you can schedule your time working through it. If you are going to use it for a ten-week book study, you will want to read the Teaching Chapter in Week 1, "The Word of the Lord," before the first meeting. (There is no Personal Bible Study section for the first week.) From then on, participants will need to come to the group time having completed the Personal Bible Study for the next week's lesson as well as having read the Teaching Chapter. You may want to put a star beside questions in the Personal Bible Study and underline key passages in the chapter that you want to be sure to bring up in the discussion. During your time together each week, you will use the Discussion Guide to talk through the big ideas of the week's lesson.

There is a great deal of material here, and you may want to take your time with it, letting its foundational truths sink in. To work your way through the study over a twenty-week period, break each week into two parts, spending one week on the Personal Bible Study section—either doing it on your own and discussing your answers when you meet or actually working through the questions together as a group. Over the following week, group members can read the chapter on their own and then come together to discuss the big ideas of the lesson.

If you are leading a group study, we would like to provide you with a leader's guide that has been developed specifically for this study. To download the free leader's guide, go to http://www.SeeingJesusinthe OldTestament.com.

My prayer for you, as you begin this study of the Prophetic Books, is that it will help you to grow in your understanding of the sovereign plan of God for his people and his outworking of that plan in history. These books help us to see that God is patient with disobedient people and merciful to those who turn and return to him, even as the books are hard on us in regard to sins we'd like to ignore. But mostly the books help us see the person at the center of God's sovereign plan—his

Son, Jesus. As I've worked my way through these Prophetic Books, they have held up a mirror that I've needed to look into, revealing sins I've needed to repent of. But they have also held up a magnifying glass to Christ, enabling me to see him in ways that have enlarged my understanding and increased my appreciation for what he accomplished when he came the first time and my longing for him to come again and complete everything these prophets promise he will do. May you see Jesus and grow in your anticipation of seeing him face-to-face as you study the Old Testament prophets.

—Nancy Guthrie

An Introduction to the Prophets

Teaching Chapter

The Word of the Lord

Do you, right now, have a smartphone within your grasp? Have you checked to see if you've had a message in the last fifteen minutes? If you're like me, you can hardly stand to see that red light blinking and not look to see what the message is. Maybe you've read or heard some of these self-tests to see if you are developing an unhealthy addiction to your device:

꙳ If you're driving around town and discover that you forgot your phone, do you find yourself becoming very unsettled about what messages you may be missing?

꙳ Have you ever almost rear-ended someone or run off the road because you were trying to read a text or type one?

꙳ Have you ever completed a transaction at a store without once speaking to the person waiting on you because you were talking on your phone?

꙳ Have you put your phone on vibrate at the movie theater or at church rather than turn it off, even though you're not expecting anything important?

꙳ Have you developed a habit of checking your phone every few minutes whether or not you've heard a tone or seen a flashing light, just in case you've missed something?

꙳ Do you find that you feel a surge of significance when you get a message and a tinge of disappointment when there are no new messages?

And here's the real kicker:

∼ Have you ever answered your phone while in the bathroom and had to delay flushing so you would not give yourself away?

Is it not embarrassing to think about how desperate we are to make sure we don't miss any messages? Someone out there—anyone out there—may have something to tell us, and we simply must know now. Sometimes our desperation to read a message is almost as if it were a message straight from God himself.

And then we realize—God has sent us a message, the most important message we will ever receive. The Bible, though written by human authors, is God speaking. And what is most amazing about the Bible is that it is not just a record of what God has said in the past. When we read the Bible, it is God actively speaking to us right now. The book of Hebrews begins with these words:

> Long ago, at many times and in many ways, *God spoke* . . . (Heb. 1:1)

I have to stop right there so that we can think about what this means: *God spoke.* Perhaps this has been drained of wonder for us. God—the God whose word has the power to call planets and plants and people into existence, who from eternity past has existed in unfathomable splendor—has condescended to distill his thundering voice into human language. This God has sent us a message about how life in his world works and why it doesn't always work well and what he has done and will do about it.

> Long ago, at many times and in many ways, God spoke to our fathers *by the prophets.* (Heb. 1:1)

Who were the prophets? The first prophet was Moses. Before Moses, God communicated directly with the heads of individual families by visions and dreams or by appearing to them and speaking. Abraham, Isaac, Jacob, and Joseph all received these kinds of personal revelations. Rather than having another person bring them the word of God, the Lord himself spoke directly to them in a variety of ways. But by Moses's day, the twelve sons of Jacob had burgeoned into a populace of six hundred thousand heads of families. How would God speak to this huge crowd of people? Through Moses, God began to speak to the nation through a spokesperson known as a prophet.

After Moses, God spoke through a number of other prophets. After Moses, the one who really catches our attention is Samuel. He prophesied during the time of the judges. Samuel as God's prophet anointed the first king of Israel, Saul, and then the great king of Israel, David. And, really, the rise or expansion of the number of prophets in Israel coincides with the rise of the monarchy in Israel.

We tend to think of Israel's kings through the lens of other kingships in history—as having absolute power. But that is not how it was supposed to work in ancient Israel. The prophet was the one who anointed and installed the king. The prophet was to stand in the counsel of God and then give direction to the king from God. Much of what the prophets said in their day to the king and to the people is written down in the Prophetic Books of the Old Testament—books that go by the prophet's name, such as Isaiah, Jeremiah, Ezekiel, Jonah, Hosea, and Micah. Over one hundred times in the Historical and Prophetic Books of the Old Testament we read that "the word of the LORD came" to a prophet. The prophets did not communicate their own ideas or agendas. They were called by God to be spokesmen for God.

And, amazingly, though the books by the prophets were God's message to his people in their day, they are no less God's message for you and me today. But can we be honest about the Prophetic Books? Aren't they, in some ways, the most difficult part of the Bible to grasp? Aren't they the books of the Bible that most of us know the least about? If I asked you to give me a sentence describing what *Lord of the Flies* or *The Scarlet Letter* or *The Adventures of Huckleberry Finn* is about, I imagine you'd be able to tell me. But, if you're like me, you'd probably have a harder time describing what the books of Micah or Ezekiel or Malachi are about, wouldn't you? Many of us would say that the Bible is the most important book in our lives, and yet there are parts of it we've been content to not really know about. But we want that to change. So, perhaps we should just deal up front with the problems we are going

to have to overcome if we want to hear God speaking to us through the
Old Testament Prophetic Books.

The Problems with the Prophets We Must Overcome

What is it that makes the Old Testament Prophetic Books difficult to
read and understand?

First, *we're unfamiliar with the history and geography.* If you or I were
reading something that had references to the Depression or 9/11 or to
the Rockies or the Big Apple, we would have no trouble understanding these references because they entail history and geography we are
familiar with. But when we read that Isaiah sees a warrior coming from
Edom in crimson garments, we don't get what this means because we
don't know that Edom represents the enemies of God and of God's people throughout the Old Testament. When Amos talks about the "cows
of Bashan" (Amos 4:1), we don't laugh out loud as we should. We don't
immediately get that those "cows" were rich, lazy women who didn't
care about the poor, because we're unfamiliar with the sociopolitical
landscape of his day.

Likewise, because most of us lack a basic mental picture of the
geography of countries and cities of the ancient Middle East, these
geographical references don't immediately register. You may not have
spent a lot of time looking at the maps at the end of your Bible. But
a little time spent with the maps will be a great help to you in grasping what is being said in the Prophetic Books. To help you with this, a
map that shows the divided kingdoms of Israel and Judah (p. 21) and
a wider map that shows Assyria and Babylonia in relation to Israel and
Judah (p. 164) have been included in this book.

I grew up going to Sunday school, learning all the stories of the Old
Testament. But as grateful as I am for this background, somehow I never
really grasped how those stories fit together. My knowledge of the history of the Old Testament was a mishmash of kings and kingdoms and
battles and exiles that I made little sense of for most of my life. Maybe
you have had the same experience. So let's take a minute to nail down
the most basic history we need to grasp to make sense of the Prophetic
Books—and, really, the whole of the story of the people of God.

The Divided Kingdoms of Israel and Judah

Remember that the Israelites came into the land as twelve tribes and eventually were given a king. There was Saul, then David, and then Solomon. After King Solomon died, the kingdom of Israel split into two kingdoms. The ten tribes in the north were called "Israel" and are sometimes referred to as "Samaria," which was the name of their capital. And the two tribes in the south—Judah and Benjamin—were called "Judah" and are sometimes referred to as "Jerusalem," which was their capital. Eventually the northern kingdom was conquered by Assyria and taken into exile and never really returned but was essentially folded into other people groups. Two hundred years later, the southern kingdom, Judah, was taken into exile in Babylon, and eventually a small remnant of those exiles from Judah returned to the land and were then known as "Jews."

Some of the prophets prophesied during the days before the northern kingdom was taken into exile. We'll start next week with Jonah, who prophesied to the northern kingdom. There are also prophets who prophesied in the southern kingdom before and after the northern kingdom went into exile. Those prophets constantly called Judah to look at what had happened in the northern kingdom to avoid the same experience. But they didn't. So we also have prophets who prophesied to the people of Judah living in exile in Babylon and a couple who prophesied to those who eventually returned to Jerusalem.

But this brings up another obstacle we have to overcome to study the Prophetic Books. You and I tend to prefer reading our history from beginning to end, in chronological order. So we might expect that the Prophetic Books that appear earlier in our Bibles were written first. But the Prophetic Books are not placed in our Bibles in chronological order, and the material within the books is not always presented in chronological order. These books were written by ancient Eastern writers who organized material differently than we do.

If you will open up your Bible to the contents page, you'll see that in the Old Testament we have the five books of Moses, from Genesis through Deuteronomy; then the Historical Books, from Joshua through Esther; and then the Wisdom Books, from Job through Song of Solomon. Following those books, we have the Major and the Minor Prophets, from

Isaiah through Malachi. We might assume that everything we read about from Isaiah through Malachi happened after what we read about in the preceding books. But in reality we can lay the content of the prophets over the content of 2 Kings, 1 and 2 Chronicles, Ezra, and Nehemiah in terms of dating. The prophets prophesied at the time of the events described in the Historical Books.

We might also assume that because Isaiah is the first of the Prophetic Books, he was the first prophet to write his book. But he wasn't. The book of Isaiah is first because it is the longest. The next book, Jeremiah, is the next longest book. The Major Prophets are major because they are longer, and the Minor Prophets are minor not because they are less important, but because they are shorter.

Because we want to grasp the historical setting these books were written in so that we can better understand their message, we're going to go in chronological order instead of biblical order. We won't be able to explore each of the sixteen Prophetic Books, but we'll cover nine of them over the course of our study.

So our unfamiliarity with ancient geography and history as well as our love for chronology makes understanding the Prophetic Books a challenge, but hopefully we're already getting a better grasp of that. A second reason we struggle to understand the Prophetic Books is that *we're easily bored or confused by their repetitive oracles.* As we work our way through the Prophetic Books, we'll see that some of them tell us a story—such as that of the prophet Jonah and that of Daniel and his friends. But much of the content in the Prophetic Books is made up of oracles. Some of the oracles are like sermons or extended poems. Others are in the form of a dialogue between the prophet and God or a description of a visionary experience given to the prophet by God. Many of the Prophetic Books are collections of oracles of a particular prophet, selected from a lifetime of prophetical ministry—kind of like a "greatest hits" album by your favorite recording artist. It can be difficult to know where one oracle ends and another begins, and the content of the oracles can seem repetitive. But recognizing and identifying these repeated elements will actually help us. There are really only three major themes, and they are reiterated throughout the Prophetic Books: sin, judgment, and hope.

The prophets weren't really telling the king and the people to do anything new. Instead, they were like prosecutors in our legal system, charging the people with crimes against God's law, the Ten Commandments. We're going to find that the prophets repeatedly pointed out the ways God's people were not obeying the commandments that had been given long before through Moses. The prophets reiterated the same promised blessings for obedience and curses for disobedience that Moses had revealed back in Deuteronomy. The prophets confronted God's people about having other gods before Yahweh, bowing down to graven images, taking the Lord's name in vain, and treating the Sabbath like any other day. The prophets indicted God's people for dishonoring their parents and for murder, adultery, theft, lying, and coveting.

But the prophets were after more than just rigid obedience to the law. They called God's people to love the Lord, which is and always has been the heart of real obedience to God's law. They point out all the things that the people loved in place of God, including: bribes (Isa. 1:23), sleep (Isa. 56:10), foreign gods (Jer. 2:25), lies (Jer. 5:31), playing the prostitute (Ezek. 23:14, 17), sacred raisin cakes of other gods (Hos. 3:1), shameful ways (Hos. 4:18), bringing offerings to centers of false worship (Amos 4:4–5), and evil (Mic. 3:2). The only cure for this wholehearted departure into sin lay in their return to an all-consuming love for the Lord.[1] That's what the prophets called them to.

A third thing that makes the Prophetic Books challenging is that *we have a misunderstanding about what prophecy is.* We tend to think of a prophet as someone who predicts the future, much like a fortune-teller or psychic. And it is true that there was an element of prediction in the Old Testament prophets' job and message. They spoke of coming judgment, the exile, and the future restoration of a faithful remnant to the land. But the prophets did not make their predictions primarily to inform the people of their day about the future; rather, the predictions were meant to encourage the people of God to form the future.[2] Their predictions were often conditional, intended to act as incentives toward repentance and obedience.

These are some of the things that make the Prophetic Books challenging to grasp, and you might think of others. So what makes them worth our investment over the weeks to come? I want to suggest several reasons we should lean in to listen to the message God gave to his people through his prophets.

The Message of the Prophets We Must Hear

The first reason we need to study the Prophetic Books is that *we struggle with the same sins they struggled with*: idolatry, disregard for God's law, empty religiosity, being in love with the world, hard-heartedness, greed, lack of concern for the poor, and presumption as members of the covenant community. If you read that list and really don't see your own sin in it, that doesn't mean this study isn't for you. In fact, it might mean that this study is even more important for you. We are so very practiced in denying our sinfulness. We rationalize and minimize and relabel our sins so that they don't even come up on our radar. Maybe you and I need to hear repeatedly about the sins that break the heart of God so that conviction will penetrate our well-rehearsed denials. Maybe, as Israel's and Judah's sins were exposed so that they might come to repentance, our sins will be exposed so that we will come to repentance.

So, first, we struggle with the same sins they struggled with, and second, *we are subject to the same judgment.* God's judgment on his people in the time of the prophets meant that they lost their inheritance in the land, they were exiled from the rest that God provided, and God's presence was withdrawn from their midst. And, my friend, we are subject to that same judgment. No one who claims to be part of the people of God yet lives in ongoing, unrepentant rebellion against the commands of God can anticipate inheriting all that God has promised or enjoying the rest that God provides. Instead, he or she can anticipate an eternity away from the presence of God.

While we struggle with the same sins and are subject to the same judgment, *we also share the same hope*—hope in God for restoration, renewal, and rest. We will see that along with the oracles pointing out sin and warning of the judgment to come, there are also oracles of hope, proclaiming the salvation to come—the same salvation we enjoy in part now and will enjoy in fullness later because *we await the same*

Savior through whom all of these hopes become reality. The people of the prophets' day looked into the future, placing all their hopes on the Messiah who would come, and they were saved. We look back, placing all our hopes on the Messiah who came, and we are saved.

That brings us to the fifth reason we should study the Prophetic Books. We should study them because *we enjoy a superior revelation*. Get this: when you read in Isaiah about the servant who will suffer, or in Ezekiel about the shepherd who will tend his flock, or in Daniel about someone "like a son of man," you can see more clearly than Isaiah or Ezekiel or Daniel the person they were writing about. Peter wrote:

> Concerning this salvation, the prophets who prophesied about the grace that was to be yours searched and inquired carefully, inquiring what person or time the Spirit of Christ in them was indicating when he predicted the sufferings of Christ and the subsequent glories. (1 Pet. 1:10–11)

Peter says that the prophets wrote about "the grace that was to be yours." What is this grace? Grace is and has always been more than a sentiment or an attitude or an action on God's part. God's grace has always centered on and flowed out of the person of Jesus Christ. Jesus said to the people of his day:

> Blessed are your eyes, because they see; and your ears, because they hear. I tell you the truth, many prophets and righteous people longed to see what you see, but they didn't see it. And they longed to hear what you hear, but they didn't hear it. (Matt. 13:16–17 NLT)

The prophets wrote beyond that which they could see and understand in the way that we can. They did not live to see the Word of the Lord who came, the Word who became flesh and dwelt among us. The Spirit of Christ spoke to them about his person and his work, his suffering and his glory, but they did not live to lay their eyes on him. In fact, after God spoke to his prophet Malachi, it seemed that God had stopped speaking. There was only silence—four hundred years of silence. Some likely gave up waiting for all that the prophets had written about to be fulfilled. But others continued to long for the day when all God's promises would become reality. At the beginning of Luke's Gospel we read:

> Now there was a man in Jerusalem, whose name was Simeon, and this man was righteous and devout, waiting for the consolation of Israel, and the Holy Spirit was upon him. And it had been revealed to him by the Holy Spirit that he would not see death before he had seen the Lord's Christ. And he came in the Spirit into the temple, and when the parents brought in the child Jesus, to do for him according to the custom of the Law, he took him up in his arms and blessed God and said, "Lord, now you are letting your servant depart in peace, according to your word; for my eyes have seen your salvation that you have prepared in the presence of all peoples, a light for revelation to the Gentiles, and for glory to your people Israel." (Luke 2:25–32)

It is this salvation, this light, this glory, this person that we will see— perhaps in a fresh way—through our study of the Old Testament prophets.

The Person in the Prophets We Must See

In our study of the Prophetic Books, *we'll see the predictions that Jesus fulfilled.* The prophets are full of specific predictions about who the Messiah would be, where he would come from, and what he would do. Isaiah wrote that a virgin would conceive and bear a son who would be called Immanuel (Matt. 1:23 cf. Isa. 7:14; 8:1, 10). That's Jesus. Micah wrote that a shepherd king would come out of Bethlehem (Mic. 5:2). That's Jesus. Zechariah told Israel to "Behold, your king coming to you . . . humble and mounted on a donkey" (Zech. 9:9), which was fulfilled when Jesus rode into Jerusalem, hailed as a king, riding on a donkey (Matt. 21:4). Isaiah wrote of one who was pierced for our rebellion, crushed for our sins, beaten so we could be whole, whipped so we could be healed (Isaiah 53). Daniel wrote of an "anointed one" who would be killed, appearing to have accomplished nothing (Daniel 9). That's Jesus.

For most of my life, if you had asked me how or where the Old Testament spoke of Christ, I would have pointed to these kinds of specific predictions regarding who the Messiah would be and things he would do. And these are so very significant. But as we work our way through the prophets, we're going to see how they point us to Jesus in other ways as well, so that Jesus could say that the whole of the Old Testament was most profoundly about him (Luke 24:27).

Second, we'll see problems that Jesus solves. The Old Testament is an unfinished book. It ends with needs that have not been met, problems that have not been solved, and tensions that have not been resolved. When we come to the end of the history recorded in the Old Testament, a small group of Israelites has returned to Jerusalem and gone to work rebuilding the city. But their capital city is not the powerful fortress it once was. They have no king on the throne like they once had in David and Solomon. They have rebuilt the temple, but it is certainly not as magnificent as the temple once was; it comes nowhere near the descriptions of the glorious temple that the prophets said would one day be in Jerusalem. God's covenant people are living in the land given to them by God, but they simply cannot live up to their part of the covenant commitment. When they do have a heart to obey, it just doesn't last.

Yet they have this word from God through the prophets that promises a greater redemption than their forefathers experienced from Egypt, greater than they experienced coming home from Babylon. They have the promises of a great city, a land of abundance to live in, a glorious temple in which God dwells, and a righteous king on the throne. So how could they reconcile the limited nature of their redemption, their city, their temple, and their covenant and king with the glorious promises made through the prophets? Jesus does that.

Jesus accomplished a far greater redemption than just returning one people group to a run-down land. His gospel is going out as his Word is preached so that he is redeeming people from every tribe and tongue to make one holy nation that will live forever with him in a glorious land. Jesus is the great king who rules over his people in perfect justice and righteousness. Jesus himself is the temple where God's people commune with God. Jesus is the better mediator of a better covenant, not only because he has written his law on our hearts by his Spirit, but also because he has taken upon himself the covenant curse for our disobedience. We're going to see how Jesus meets the needs, solves the problems, and resolves the tensions left unanswered, unsolved, and unresolved throughout the Old Testament.

Third, we'll see people in whom Jesus was prefigured. Ever since Moses wrote, "The LORD your God will raise up for you a prophet like me from among you, from your brothers—it is to him you shall listen" (Deut. 18:15), the people of God looked for and waited for that great prophet. Many of the prophets God sent provided glimpses of the great prophet he would one day send. Jeremiah, in his weeping over the sin of his people and the judgment to come because of that sin, prefigured Jesus, who wept over the city of Jerusalem, which would not repent and turn to him. Hosea, as the bridegroom paying the ransom so that he could bring home his unfaithful bride to love and cleanse, prefigured Jesus, who paid the ransom so that he might bring us home to God. Jonah's three days in the belly of a great fish provided a picture that Jesus himself called upon to point to the three days he would spend in the belly of the earth.

"Long ago, at many times and in many ways, God spoke to our fathers by the prophets," we've read in Hebrews 1, and it continues: "but in these last days he has spoken to us by his Son" (Heb. 1:1–2). Jesus was the great prophet that all the prophets pointed to. Yet he was not just a messenger declaring a message from God—he is the message.

Finally, we'll see a pattern that Jesus superseded. There is a pattern in the Old Testament—the pattern of God's having a son put to the test of obedience to his word. Understanding this pattern helps us to make sense not just of the Prophetic Books but of the whole Bible. In Genesis we read that God created the world and made man, male and female, in his image and put them in the garden he had created so that they would obey his word and enjoy his blessing and be fruitful and multiply so that his world would be filled with human beings, enjoying his creation, his blessings, and his presence with them. But Adam, this first son, was disobedient and was expelled from God's land of Eden.

But God did not abandon his purpose; instead his purpose became a promise. The pattern was repeated as God called a people to himself and brought them out of the chaos and bondage of Egypt to live in the land he provided. There they were to be a kingdom of priests, enjoying his blessing and obeying the Word he had given them at Mount Sinai. He gave them a king to rule over them and came down to dwell among them in the temple. And for a time, it was almost like his people were back in the garden of Eden, as they enjoyed God's blessing and his presence in the Promised Land. But it didn't last. When we come to the time of the prophets, we find this son, the nation of Israel, rebelling and refusing to obey God's Word, just as Adam did in the garden. Like Adam, they found themselves under God's judgment, exiled from the land that God had given to them, a small refugee community in Babylon. They lost their land, their king, their temple, and their city, and, as far as they were concerned, they had lost their God.

But God clearly had not abandoned them. He was still speaking through his prophets, promising them that he would repeat the pattern again. But this time he would do it in a way that could not be ruined by human sin. There would be another son, the second Adam, the true Israel. He would obey rather than rebel. He would make a new covenant. He would bring a new city in which he would be the king and the temple. What God intended to do through him would be on a whole new scale. It wouldn't be confined to one family or one nation. It would be for the benefit of all the peoples of the world.

As we study the prophets, we can never think that the exiles' returning to the land, putting a monarch on a throne, or rebuilding the temple was the fulfillment of all God promised through his prophets. Those things were only partial fulfillment. Nor can we think that their physical descendants, the Jewish people of today, being regathered to a particular piece of real estate and rebuilding a temple made of limestone in which animal sacrifices are reinstituted, is something to anticipate as a fulfillment of God's promises through his prophets. God's intention has always been to far surpass those limited physical blessings and to bless us "in Christ with every spiritual blessing in the heavenly places" (Eph. 1:3). The pattern has been superseded by Jesus and will not regress to merely physical fulfillments. "For all the promises of God find their Yes in him" (2 Cor. 1:20).

There is so much to see of Jesus in the books we are about to study, and I hope your eyes are peeled to take it all in.

 ⌒ In Jonah we'll see by contrast the compassion of Jesus, who ran toward those under judgment rather than away from them.

∼ In Hosea we'll see Jesus as our faithful bridegroom, who paid the price of his own blood to redeem us, his unfaithful bride, from our slavery to sin.

∼ In Micah we'll see the humble justice and mercy of Jesus as the one whose life and death answers Micah's difficult question: "What does the LORD require?" (6:8).

∼ In Isaiah we'll see Jesus as the divine King seated on the throne Isaiah saw in the year King Uzziah died, as the suffering servant who will be punished in place of his people, and as the coming conqueror who will put an end to evil.

∼ In Habakkuk we'll see that Jesus is the one by whom sinful, faithless people are credited the righteousness needed to live by faith.

∼ In Jeremiah we'll see Jesus finally fulfilling God's promise of a new covenant that will implant in us a heart that wants to obey.

∼ In Daniel we'll see Jesus as the glorious Son of Man who has received from the Ancient of Days a kingdom that will never oppress and never pass away.

∼ In Ezekiel we'll see the promised presence of Jesus with us, never to leave us, in a new city called "The LORD is There" (48:35).

∼ And, finally, in Malachi, as we consider the question, "Who can stand when he appears?" (3:2) we'll see Jesus, who makes it possible for us to say with confidence, "I will be able to stand when he appears—not because I am clean or good or worthy in myself, but because the Word of the Lord who came has come to me and made me his own."

Over and over again in the prophets we'll read that "the word of the Lord came to" his prophet. And when we read these words, we will recognize the voice of this Word, the Word who was with God, the Word who was God, the Word that became flesh and dwelt among us, the only Son from the Father, full of grace and truth (John 1:1, 14). We'll know that Christ was speaking not only to the prophets and not only to the people in the prophets' day, but also to us, revealing himself to us in new ways, calling us to himself in fresh and perhaps costly ways, and promising himself to us in saving ways.

Discussion Guide

An Introduction to the Prophets

Getting the Discussion Going

1. Nancy mentioned several things that make studying the Prophetic Books challenging: the fact that we are unfamiliar with the historical and geographical setting, that the oracles are repetitive and confusing, and that we misunderstand the nature of prophecy. Can you relate to any of those, or are there other aspects of the Prophetic Books that you find intimidating or challenging?

2. Many of us have Bibles that include maps to help us with the geography, and timelines of the kings and prophets to help us with the flow of history. Let's take a minute to look in our Bibles to see and share with each other what resources we might have at our fingertips to help us overcome this challenge to studying the Prophetic Books. (For example, on page 1232 of the *ESV Study Bible*, there is a timeline entitled "Activity of the Writing Prophets during the Reigns of the Kings of Israel and Judah." In the back, map 6 displays the divided kingdom, and map 7 displays the Assyrian and Babylonian Empires that took Israel and Judah into exile.)

Getting to the Heart of It

3. While the priests in Israel were all from the tribe of Levi, and the kings descended from other kings, none of the prophets became a prophet

because his father was a prophet. Some of the prophets were priests, but most were ordinary people called by God in a variety of ways, from a variety of backgrounds, to speak for God. Read the following verses and note the different ways God called and instructed his prophets.

~ Isaiah 6:1–9
~ Jeremiah 1:1–9
~ Ezekiel 1:1–3; 2:1–3; 3:27
~ Hosea 1:2
~ Amos 7:14–15
~ Jonah 1:1

4. In 2 Peter 1:21 we read: "For no prophecy was ever produced by the will of man, but men spoke from God as they were carried along by the Holy Spirit." How does this help to explain why the content of the Prophetic Books is somewhat repetitive and never contradictory, although it varies in style and setting?

5. Turn to 1 Peter 1:10–12. Discuss what these verses reveal about:

~ the subject of the Prophetic Books
~ the limits to the prophets' understanding
~ the source of the prophets' message
~ the specifics of what was revealed
~ the reason the prophets wrote down their prophecy

Getting Personal
6. What did you read or hear in the teaching that helps you to believe that what the prophets had to say to the people of their day might also speak to you today? And what do you think is required for you to hear that message?

Getting How It Fits into the Big Picture
7. We're going to see, as we work our way through the Prophetic Books, that much of what the prophets said was going to happen, did hap-

pen shortly after the prophecy was given. Some of it was fulfilled in the incarnation, ministry, death, and resurrection of Christ. Some of it is being fulfilled now as the gospel of Christ brings life to peoples and nations throughout the earth. And some of it is yet to be fulfilled, when Christ returns to establish the new heaven and the new earth. What does this tell us about the value of studying the message of the prophets?

Week 2

Jonah

Personal Bible Study

Jonah

To get a sense of the geography of this story before you begin to study it, find the key cities mentioned in the story of Jonah on a map, including: Joppa, Tarshish, and Nineveh.

The Setting of Jonah

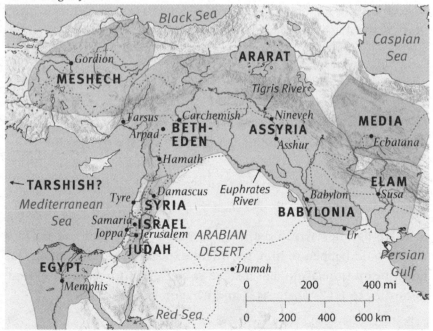

1. Read Jonah 1:1–2. What two things did God tell Jonah to do and why?

2. Read Jonah 1:3–16. What did the captain tell Jonah to do, and do you find any evidence that he did it?

3. In Jonah 1:8, the sailors ask Jonah a series of questions, and his answer is found in verse 9. What is interesting about his answer, considering the situation he was in?

4. According to Jonah 1:11–13, what did Jonah tell the sailors to do so that the storm would stop, and what did they do instead?

5. The sailors, who had all been praying to their gods for help, did something amazing. According to Jonah 1:14–16, what was it?

6. If we had never read the story of Jonah before and had no idea what would happen to him, we might expect to read that Jonah was never heard from again. But instead something surprising happened. According to 1:17, what was it, and what or who caused it?

7. Jonah 2 is written in the form of a psalm, describing Jonah's prayer to God in his distress. Consider that Jonah may have written this later as he reflected on his desperate prayer and miraculous salvation rather than this being a record of the text of his prayer from inside the fish. According to verses 2–7 write phrases that indicate:

What Jonah did:

What God did:

8. Jonah's prayer psalm ends with a statement that is likely intended to be the crescendo or key point of his entire book: "Salvation belongs to the Lord!" (2:9). Some theologians say that this could actually be the key point or summary message of the entire Bible. How has this truth been evident in Jonah 1 and 2; and, from what you know of Jonah's story, how will it also prove true in Jonah 3 and 4?

9. Read Jonah 3:1–4. In these verses we have the entire sermon Jonah preached or at least a concise summary of his message. What is it?

10. According to Jonah 3:5–8, how did the people of Nineveh respond to Jonah's sermon?

11. According to Jonah 3:10, how did God respond to the real change in the lives of the people of Nineveh, and how is this a demonstration of the truth found in Jeremiah 18:7–10?

12. If we were writing Jonah's story, we would probably end it differently from what we read in Jonah 4. We would like it to end with Jonah celebrating that God had turned away his wrath from the Ninevites after they repented. But Jonah's response was very different. According to Jonah 4:1–3, what was it and why?

13. How is the way Jonah felt when God showed mercy to the Ninevites different from how he felt when God showed him mercy by sending the great fish to save him?

14. Read Jonah 4:4–11. What point do you think God is making to Jonah by providing a plant for shade and then sending a worm to destroy the plant?

15. Jesus told the scribes and Pharisees that the people of Nineveh repented when Jonah preached but that someone "greater than Jonah" was preaching to them, and they did not repent (Matt. 12:38-41). Let's consider some ways that Jesus is "greater than Jonah." Read the following statements about Jonah and write a corresponding or contrasting statement about Jesus, following the examples given for the first two. The statement about Jesus should be worded similarly to the statement about Jonah.

Jonah	Jesus
"The word of the LORD came to Jonah." (1:1)	John 1:14 *Jesus is the Word of the Lord who came.*
Jonah was sent by God to deliver a message of condemnation to a people deserving judgment. (1:2)	John 3:17 *Jesus was sent by God to deliver a message of salvation to a people deserving judgment.*
When God called Jonah to go to Nineveh, Jonah turned and went in the other direction. (1:3)	Luke 9:43–44, 51–53
Because he had been disobedient to God, Jonah offered himself up to die in the sea so that everyone on the ship would live. (1:12)	Heb. 7:27
A guilty Jonah was thrown off the ship to die by sailors who said, "LORD, don't make us die [changed from "pay"] for this man's sin." (1:14 NLT)	Matt. 20:28; Heb. 9:28
Jonah was in the belly of the fish three days and three nights before being vomited onto dry land. (1:17)	Matt. 12:40

Jonah was powerless to save his own life at the bottom of the sea and in the belly of the fish. (2:6)	John 10:18
Jonah preached to Gentiles who were quick to repent. (3:4–5)	Matt. 11:20
Jonah was angry as he looked over the city that repented and was saved. (4:1, 5)	Luke 19:41–42
Jonah wanted to die rather than live in a world where people he hated experienced God's mercy. (4:3)	Eph. 2:3–5

Teaching Chapter

Questions God Asks

I suppose professional counselors in training pay a lot of money to educational institutions to learn how to ask good questions—questions that help us to think more deeply about our motivations and desires. I can remember sitting across from a counselor one time who asked me, "What are you afraid of?" Exploring the answer to that question helped me to unearth the real issue I had to deal with that was making me miserable at the time. I, myself, am not a great counselor. However, I have been known to channel Dr. Phil and respond to someone by asking, "So how's that working for you?" It's a good question. In fact, it seems like the kind of question God might ask. When we work our way through the Scriptures, we discover that God asks very good questions—questions that uncover the real issues in the lives of the people he loves.

The first question God asks in the Bible is found in Genesis 3 when he called to Adam, saying, "Where are you?" and then to the woman, asking, "What is this that you have done?" (Gen. 3:9, 13). Of course God knew where Adam and Eve were hiding and exactly what they'd done. He wanted Adam and Eve to face the reality of what they had done and where it had taken them. Later, when elderly Sarah laughed after overhearing God tell Abraham that she was going to give birth to a son, God asked, "Why did Sarah laugh and say, 'Shall I indeed bear a child, now that I am old?' Is anything too hard for the LORD?" (Gen. 18:13–14). The unbelief underneath Sarah's skeptical laugh needed to be brought to the surface to be dealt with. Wrestling with Jacob in the dark, God asked him, "What is your name?" (Gen. 32:27). Certainly God knew his name. This was a call for confession, as just saying his name, which meant "cheater" or "swindler," gave Jacob the opportunity to come clean. Each time God asks a question in the Bible, we know it is not because he does not know the answer to the question. Clearly he wants the person being questioned to examine what is really going on in his or her heart.

We're going to hear God ask some challenging questions as we work our way through the Prophetic Books, beginning with the book of Jonah. For most of us, this is a familiar story. We've read the picture-book version to our kids that focuses on the big fish. We know the series of events that make up this book. But what is this book really about? What were the people of Jonah's day supposed to take away from this book, which is really Jonah's confession? If we can find an answer to that question, we'll be able to figure out what you and I are intended to take away from this book. And I promise you that it has very little to do with a big fish. That big fish is really just a bit player in a far bigger drama.

Jonah's Rebellion

The book of Jonah begins with the Lord entrusting a message to his prophet:

> Now the word of the LORD came to Jonah the son of Amittai. (Jonah 1:1)

Jonah was a prophet in Israel, the northern kingdom, in the time after the united kingdom divided. We know this because Jonah is also mentioned in 2 Kings 14, where we discover that he prophesied to the northern kingdom of Israel and that he was the rare prophet who got to deliver a word of good news. Jonah prophesied that territory that had been lost to Israel's northern enemies was going to come back under Israelite control, and the prophecy proved true. So we can imagine that Jonah was popular in a way that most prophets were not, a popularity he probably enjoyed. But then the word of the Lord came to Jonah, telling him to take God's message outside Israel's borders:

> Arise, go to Nineveh, that great city, and call out against it, for their evil
> has come up before me. (Jonah 1:2)

Jonah must have thought, *Surely I didn't hear that right. I'm a prophet to
Israel. I speak for God to God's covenant people, not to Gentiles, and certainly not to Ninevites.* In Jonah's day there was one world superpower—
the Assyrians. For generations Assyria had been making fierce raids
on the lands bordering the Mediterranean, including Israel. Having
refined the art of torture, they were known for their brutality. Evidently
their evil had not escaped the notice of God himself. He wanted Jonah
to go to Nineveh, an enormous city in the middle of Assyria, to declare
his coming judgment.

> But Jonah rose to flee to Tarshish, away from the presence of the LORD.
> (Jonah 1:3)

Jonah took off in the exact opposite direction from Nineveh. Why
didn't Jonah want to go to Nineveh? Was it just the inconvenience of
a long journey? It couldn't have been that, because he was willing to
journey to Tarshish, which was considered the end of the earth at that
point in time. Was it that he was afraid? Certainly he had cause to be
afraid. If you go to the British Museum in London, you can see huge
stone panels that once decorated the rooms and courtyards in the
king's palace in Assyria. These panels depict the various ways they tortured their enemies. This was their idea of decorating the living room.
So certainly, marching into Nineveh with a message of God's disap-
proval did sound like a plum prophetical assignment.

However, knowing that they were such a threat, I would think that
Jonah would have liked the message he was given to deliver: he was
to "call out against it." If Nineveh was destroyed, the Israelites could
breathe a huge sigh of relief. Jonah was a man who loved his country,
and, for him, that meant that he hated Israel's enemies. We could easily
imagine Jonah daydreaming about getting home from his trip and telling everyone that, sure enough, forty days after he'd called out against
it, God rained down fire on their evil enemies. But evidently that's *not*
what Jonah pictured in his mind as the outcome of his journey. If we

want to know the real reason that Jonah did not want to go and give God's message to Nineveh, he states it clearly in chapter 4:

> That is why I made haste to flee to Tarshish; for I knew that you are a gracious God and merciful, slow to anger and abounding in steadfast love, and relenting from disaster. (v. 2)

It's not so much what Jonah knew about Nineveh that made him run in the other direction. It's what he knew about God. He really believed what God had said about himself and had demonstrated again and again in Israel's history: he is a God who loves to show mercy when people repent. Jonah knew that if God wanted him to go and speak his word to the Ninevites, it was because God intended to bring the Ninevites to repentance in order that he might save them. And, frankly, Jonah did not want God to save the Ninevites. He wanted God to wipe those people off the face of the earth so that his own people, the Israelites, would not have to live in fear of them. So he hung up his prophetic credentials and headed west instead of east.

But God (and isn't that always how the story of salvation starts, "but God . . ."?) was so committed to showing mercy to the Ninevites that he not only called his prophet to go but also put a storm in his prophet's pathway that would halt his flight in the other direction. God hurled a great wind onto the Mediterranean Sea so that the ship Jonah was fleeing on would break apart in the storm. All of the sailors cried out to their gods, yet Jonah had no interest in calling out to his God for mercy. He had no interest in opening up the communication lines again with God; he was done with communicating with and for God.

The pagan soldiers wrote the names of everyone onboard on small pieces of wood and threw them like dice to see whose name would come up, anticipating that it would indicate which person on the ship had angered his god; and sure enough, Jonah's name came up. When they questioned Jonah, they found out that his god was the God of heaven, the God who made the sea and the dry land, and at that moment they wanted a whole lot less sea and a whole lot more dry land.

We have to wonder why Jonah didn't drop to his knees right then and beg God to still the storm. But evidently death was preferable to Jonah than calling on God, which he knew would require obeying God. So he told the sailors to throw him into the sea, assuring them that once they did, the storm would be stilled; God's wrath would be abated by the sacrifice of the one who was guilty.

But these pagan sailors didn't want Jonah to sacrifice himself for them. They seem to have had more compassion than God's prophet. They determined to row harder in the storm, thinking that they had it in their own strength to emerge from the storm of God's judgment unscathed, apart from a sacrifice, just like lots of people do today. But they couldn't do it. Finally they gave up and threw Jonah into the water. The storm stopped, and they knew Jonah's God was the true God. And though they had only just heard about Yahweh from arguably the world's worst witness, they threw themselves upon God's mercy and acknowledged their complete dependence upon him. They left their pagan gods behind and became believers in Yahweh.

The story of Jonah could have easily ended right there, with Jonah never heard from again. But God. God had worked a miracle of salvation, bringing these pagan sailors to himself, and he was about to do another one in the life of his reluctant prophet.

Jonah's Resurrection

The scene shifts from the deck of the ship to the depths of the ocean. In Jonah 2:3, Jonah describes his initial experience at the surface of the water, struggling to breathe with the waves and billows passing over him. Then he says, "The waters closed in over me to take my life" (v. 5). Jonah sank down to the bottom of the sea with seaweed firmly wrapped around his head. He recounts, "My life was fainting away" (v. 7). We've sensed Jonah sinking down and down from even before he hit the water. He began as a respected prophet, hearing the word of the Lord and delivering it to God's people, and he sank down to resigned prophet, going "down to Joppa," refusing to call out to the Lord. He went down into the ship and went to sleep, and then he sank down to the bottom of the sea. At this low place, with no more oxygen, no more energy, no more options, he finally cried out to God. He writes, "I remembered the

LORD and my prayer came to you" (2:7). God's answer came not in the form of a lecture but in the form of a fish:

> The LORD appointed a great fish to swallow up Jonah. And Jonah was in the belly of the fish three days and three nights. (Jonah 1:17)

We don't know what Jonah's time inside the fish was like—if it was comfortable and quiet or tempestuous and terrifying. But we do know that in the fish, God's prophet was finally ready to pray.

> And the LORD spoke to the fish, and it vomited Jonah out upon the dry land. (Jonah 2:10)

Jonah then went up: up from the belly of Sheol (2:2), the place of the dead, inside the fish, and onto the shore. Certainly this experience had an impact on Jonah, though we're not sure how much. We can't help but notice that his prayer of chapter 2 does not include any confession of his sin. Perhaps that's why the fish vomited Jonah out. Let's face it: the whole idea of vomit is disgusting. Perhaps God was disgusted with the stubborn self-obsession of his prophet, even though he did intend to use him.

We don't know if Jonah went home for a while to recuperate and sometime later heard the word of the Lord again, or if he heard the Lord tell him a second time to go to Nineveh the minute he hit the beach. Clearly, something was happening in Jonah's heart because this time, "Jonah arose and went to Nineveh, according to the word of the LORD" (Jonah 3:3). But we have to wonder if his heart was really in it.

> Now Nineveh was an exceedingly great city, three days' journey in breadth. Jonah began to go into the city, going a day's journey. And he called out, "Yet forty days, and Nineveh shall be overthrown!" (Jonah 3:3–4)

Picture this: the city took three days to cross, but Jonah went only as far as one day's journey in. It appears that he was not yet to the center of the huge metropolis, but he stopped and did his duty. Who knows how many could hear him? His sermon, or at least his summary of it, is just five words long in Hebrew, eight words long in our English version: "Yet forty days, and Nineveh shall be overthrown!" Maybe he cried out his simple sermon all along the way. Or maybe he just lingered on the outskirts of the city and said it in such a way that few could hear it. We are given no evidence of tears in his eyes, no evidence of pleading in his voice for the people to repent. Yet God is not hindered in his saving work by an apathetic prophet or a poor presentation. It was not the force of the argument presented or the emotion expressed by the prophet that moved the people. God's word accomplished what God intended, which it always does. And we get to witness another miracle of salvation.

Nineveh's Repentance

> And the people of Nineveh believed God. (Jonah 3:5)

There was no lengthy process of a spiritual pilgrimage, no season of getting their intellectual questions answered, no long prayers. They simply believed God. They believed what God revealed to them about the seriousness of their sin, and evidently it broke their hearts.

> They called for a fast and put on sackcloth, from the greatest of them to the least of them. (Jonah 3:5)

Jonah 3:6 says that "the word reached the king of Nineveh." Evidently Jonah didn't bother to go all the way to the palace, but his message got there anyway. And instead of being met with cynicism or anger or derision or defiance, his message was received with humility and responded to in repentance and hope. The king removed his robe, covered himself with sackcloth, and sat in ashes, revealing his sadness over his people's sin. The whole city turned their backs on the violence and cruelty that had been the fabric of their lives. That's repentance. And amazingly they dared to hope. Even though Jonah had told them that Nineveh was going to be overthrown, the king said, "Who knows? God may turn and relent and turn from his fierce anger, so that we may not perish" (v. 9).

Jonah had told them that Nineveh was going to be destroyed. So what gave them any sense of hope that God might show them mercy? Perhaps it was what they witnessed in God's prophet. The New Testament says that Jonah became "a sign" to the people of Nineveh (Luke 11:30). Perhaps Jonah's reputation, as "that guy who was swallowed by a big fish and was then spit up on the shore" preceded him all the way to Nineveh. Or perhaps Jonah told them about the mercy God had showed to him when he was caught in the storm of God's judgment, and that is what gave the Ninevites hope that God would, perhaps, show mercy to them too.

> When God saw what they did, how they turned from their evil way, God relented of the disaster that he had said he would do to them, and he did not do it. (Jonah 3:10)

In one way this is surprising, but in another way it shouldn't surprise us. This is the third time in this short book of Jonah that someone has cried out to God, and God has shown mercy. The pagan sailors cried out to him on the ship, and they were saved. Jonah cried out to God from the belly of the fish, and he was saved. Then Nineveh cried out to God, and they were saved. The surprising truth of the Bible is not so much that a big fish can swallow a man but that wicked people can be moved by God's word to repent and that God's mercy is available to *anyone* who believes—even those with blood on their hands.

When we read that God relented, it can sound to us, at first, as if God changed his mind. And that doesn't fit with what we know about God: we know that he does not change. What we must understand is that God relented because Nineveh repented. God always responds with mercy to people who repent and believe, to those who cry out to him for mercy. That is something about him that never changes. When Nineveh believed God's word and cried out for God's mercy, when they turned from all their evil, they were no longer the same Nineveh and no longer the target of God's wrath.

Jesus said that the angels rejoice in heaven when one sinner repents. Can you imagine the fireworks in heaven when 120,000 people repented? Think of the faithful preachers of God's Word throughout the ages who have labored in places with little response over a lifetime of ministry. Jonah spent one day in Nineveh, gave a five-word sermon, and 120,000 repented! If we were judging by sheer numbers or return on effort invested, we'd have to say that perhaps Jonah went from being the worst witness in the world to the greatest evangelist in history!

Once again, the story could end here. The Word of the Lord had come to Nineveh through his prophet Jonah. Nineveh had repented, and God had shown himself to be true to his character, full of mercy. We'd like to say that all lived happily forever after. But then we get to chapter 4—the part of the story that we usually skip when we're teaching children's Sunday school because we find it so inconvenient and perplexing.

Jonah's Resentment

> Jonah went out of the city and sat to the east of the city and made a booth for himself there. He sat under it in the shade, till he should see what would become of the city. (Jonah 4:5)

Evidently Jonah delivered his minimum of a message and then went outside the city to a place where he would be able to witness the devastation of God's judgment falling on Nineveh. It would seem that he didn't stick around to witness their repentance or to participate in their fasting and calling out to God. He hoped to see sulfur and fire raining down on Nineveh just as it had centuries before on Sodom and Gomorrah (Gen. 18:20; 19:24). But it didn't happen. One would think that the prophet, who had traveled all this way, would have been happy at the response to his message. One would think that after walking through the city and witnessing the darkness of life in Nineveh, Jonah's heart would have been full of relief and gratitude that the people had been delivered, not just from judgment but from their former violent way of life. But Jonah was not at all happy, or relieved, or grateful. He was just mad.

> But it displeased Jonah exceedingly, and he was angry. And he prayed to the Lord and said, "O Lord, is not this what I said when I was yet in my country? That is why I made haste to flee to Tarshish; for I knew that you are a gracious God and merciful, slow to anger and abounding in steadfast love, and relenting from disaster. Therefore now, O Lord, please take my life from me, for it is better for me to die than to live." (Jonah 4:1-3)

Jonah would rather have died than go back to Israel to report that
Nineveh had been saved. He would rather have died than relate to the
Ninevites as fellow believers in Yahweh. He would rather have died
than live in a world in which he did not get to decide who is and who
isn't worthy of God's mercy. It was at this point that God, the gracious,
wise counselor who cares for his angry prophet, asked Jonah a question intended to help him see into his own heart:

> The LORD said, "Do you do well to be angry?" (Jonah 4:4)

God challenged Jonah to refuse to allow his anger to go unexamined.
He asked the question so that Jonah would interrogate his feelings
rather than accept or deny them. Anger is a good barometer of something going on beneath the surface in our hearts. Whenever we feel
anger, we need to ask ourselves these questions: Why am I angry? Do I
do well to be angry? What expectation about how things should work
in my world is serving to justify this anger? What does my anger right
now say about what or whom I really value, what or whom I really care
about? Does the fact that I am so angry about this reveal that a good
thing may have become an ultimate thing in my life, or, in other words,
an idol?

If Jonah would examine himself in that way, it would explain what
was going on in his heart. It would expose that his heart toward the
Ninevites was nothing like God's heart toward the Ninevites. God did
more, however, than simply ask the question. In his sovereign power
he set up a scenario that would further help Jonah to face up to his
ugly inner reality, a situation that would punctuate the stark contrast
between his heart and God's heart.

> Now the LORD God appointed a plant and made it come up over Jonah,
> that it might be a shade over his head, to save him from his discomfort.
> So Jonah was exceedingly glad because of the plant. But when dawn came
> up the next day, God appointed a worm that attacked the plant, so that
> it withered. When the sun rose, God appointed a scorching east wind,
> and the sun beat down on the head of Jonah so that he was faint. And he
> asked that he might die and said, "It is better for me to die than to live."
> (Jonah 4:6–8)

Notice that the Lord caused the plant to grow "to save [Jonah] from his discomfort" and that it made Jonah "exceedingly glad." In chapter 1 we saw that Jonah was most concerned about his own country. In chapter 2 we saw that Jonah was most concerned about his continued survival. And here, in chapter 4, we see that he was most concerned about his own comfort. He did not care that about 120,000 people were facing the fires of God's judgment, but heaven forbid he get a sunburn! We read it and wonder how he could be so concerned about his own comfort while caring so little about perishing people. But as we linger, and as the Word of the Lord in this book of Jonah comes to us, it asks us, like a skilled counselor, *What do you really care about?*

Of course there is nothing wrong with caring about your comfort, but do you care so much about it that it has squeezed out any room in your life, in your heart, in your thoughts, in your schedule, or in your checkbook to care about people who will perish unless someone speaks God's Word to them, even if it is not a perfect presentation? Would an examination of what makes you really mad and what makes you really glad reveal how much you truly care or do not care about the people who live not far away in Nineveh but in your own neighborhood, people who are not strangers but are in your own family, who, right now, face a future of being under God's angry judgment? Where is the evidence in your life that you genuinely care?

In our introduction to the prophets, we asked why we should read and study these books. And for me, at least, I'm getting the first in what I hope will be a series of significant answers to that question. The reason I need to read and study the book of Jonah, the story of this prophet who doesn't care, is that it forces me to see that I don't care, at least not anywhere near the way I care about my own comfort.

God asked Jonah a question that would reveal the true nature of Jonah's heart, and the book ends with God asking a question that reveals the true nature of his own heart:

> God said to Jonah, "Do you do well to be angry for the plant?" And he said, "Yes, I do well to be angry, angry enough to die." And the LORD said, "You

pity the plant, for which you did not labor, nor did you make it grow, which came into being in a night and perished in a night. And *should not I pity Nineveh*, that great city, in which there are more than 120,000 persons who do not know their right hand from their left, and also much cattle?" (Jonah 4:9–11)

The book of Jonah ends in this untidy way, with this unanswered question. Surely readers in Jonah's day, Israelites who saw themselves as the exclusive beneficiaries of Yahweh's mercy, needed to allow this question, "Should not I pity Nineveh?" to linger. They needed to expand their understanding of the targets of God's mercy beyond their own borders. They needed to see the Ninevites not as their enemies but as people who "do not know their right hand from their left." In other words, they needed to see the Ninevites as people created in the image of God who had no direction, no ability to find their way to God. And they needed to see themselves as God had always intended them to be—a conduit of blessing to all the families of the earth.

The story of Jonah ends by showing us the stark contrast between what Jonah cared about and what God cared about. Jonah cared about his own comfort under the shady vine, which had been threatened by the worm. God cared about 120,000 people facing an eternity where the worm does not die and the fire is not quenched (Isa. 66:24). There is no clear or tidy resolution regarding the prophet Jonah. We're left with the impression of a far-from-impressive prophet. Perhaps that was so those who read his book would recognize the need for a greater prophet, a prophet who was greater than Jonah. What was really needed was not just a prophet who received the word of the Lord, but a prophet who *is* the Word of the Lord. What was needed was a prophet who would run toward sinners who need to repent, not away from them, a prophet who was not stingy with salvation but generous, "not wishing that any should perish, but that all should reach repentance" (2 Pet. 3:9). What was needed was not just a prophet who would call the ancient city of Nineveh to repentance but one who "commands all people everywhere to repent" (Acts 17:30).

Someone Greater Than Jonah

Of all the Old Testament prophets, Jonah is the only one with whom Jesus chose to directly compare himself. When the people of Jesus's day wanted to see some sort of miraculous sign that would prove to them that he was the Messiah, even though Jesus had done many, many miracles among them already, Jesus pointed to the prophet Jonah:

> Only an evil, adulterous generation would demand a miraculous sign; but the only sign I will give them is the sign of the prophet Jonah. For as Jonah was in the belly of the great fish for three days and three nights, so will the Son of Man be in the heart of the earth for three days and three nights. (Matt. 12:39–40 NLT)

Certainly the Jews who heard his answer were perplexed. They knew the story of Jonah. They must have wondered what Jonah could possibly have to do with their desire to see Jesus work a miracle. Using the familiar story of Jonah, Jesus was drawing his listeners a picture that would show them exactly what he came to do—in fact, the greatest work he would do. As Jonah went down into the pit of death, so Jesus would descend into the pit of death. And just as the fish could not contain Jonah and coughed him up, so the grave would not contain Jesus. Death's claim on Jesus would have a limit of three days. Jesus gave us the sign of Jonah by his resurrection, the sign of miraculous, unstoppable life and absolute authority over death.

But while Jesus told the people of his day that he would give them the sign of Jonah, he did not intend for them to focus on Jonah, because he continued, saying, "Someone greater than Jonah is here" Matt. 12:41 NLT). And, I wonder, if Jonah were here with us today, if he might say to us, "Read my story and see the lengths to which our God goes to save wicked people who have no idea who he is or how to find him. Read my story and see how far God goes to save rebellious sons and daughters who would rather die than be obedient. But then look at Jesus, look at the one who is greater than me, and begin to pray, *Lord, make me less like Jonah and more like Jesus.*"[3]

∾ When God asked Jonah to leave his comfortable home to go to Nineveh, a place filled with people who deserved his judgment, Jonah said no. But when God asked Jesus to leave the splendor of heaven to go to earth, a place filled with people who deserve his judgment, to take that judgment upon himself, Jesus said yes. When Jesus wrestled with what this mission would cost, he said, "I want your will to be done, not mine" (Matt. 26:39 NLT).

Perhaps you want to pray the prayer pastor Colin Smith suggests that we pray when we examine the story of Jonah, which is: *Lord, make me less like Jonah and more like Jesus.*[4] *Create in me a heart that quickly and gladly says yes to you!*

~ Jonah wanted to die because his hatred for the Assyrians was so great. But Jesus was willing to die because his love for sinners was so great.

Lord, make me less like Jonah and more like Jesus. My heart is full of my own prejudices and preferences. Give me a heart to love even my enemies as you do.

~ When God told Jonah to go to Nineveh, a place where he could have become a victim of brutal torture in the cause of salvation, Jonah turned and ran in the opposite direction. But Jesus "set his face to go to Jerusalem" (Luke 9:51), where he knew he would be brutally beaten and tortured in accomplishing salvation.

Lord, make me less like Jonah and more like Jesus. Make me willing to go wherever you send me, willing to be mistreated for your gospel. Allow me the joy of sharing in the fellowship of the suffering of Jesus.

~ Jonah cared about his own country, his own continued survival, and his own comfort, and he simply did not care about 120,000 souls who were facing an eternity of judgment. But Jesus left the comfort of his heavenly country knowing that he would be rejected and killed by the very ones he came to save.

Lord, make me less like Jonah and more like Jesus. I'm ashamed of my lack of compassion for those around me, and I seem to have no power to work it up in myself. As I get involved in the lives of others instead of retreating to a holy huddle, will you cause your compassion to overflow in me and through me?

~ Jonah was angry over God's mercy for sinners and happy about a plant that preserved his own comfort. But Jesus was angry over the hard-heartedness of religious people, and "the joy that was set before him" that enabled him to endure the cross (Heb. 12:2) was people like you and me, people from every tribe and nation of the earth saved from judgment for an eternity in his presence.

Lord, make me less like Jonah and more like Jesus. Give me insight into my anger as well as into my joy so that I can hate what you hate and love what you love.

~ Jonah preferred to die rather than to live in a world in which people he hated experienced God's mercy. But Jesus was willing to die so that people in the world whom God loves can experience his mercy.

Lord, make me less like Jonah and more like Jesus. Keep me from becoming a cold-hearted, moralistic person. Break my heart like your heart is broken for those who are perishing. Give me tears in my eyes like the tears in your eyes. May my life be a sign pointing people to you, instilling hope that you will show them the same mercy you have shown to me.

You and I were once like Jonah.

I was sinking deep in sin, far from the peaceful shore,
Very deeply stained within, sinking to rise no more;
But the Master of the sea heard my despairing cry,
From the waters lifted me, now safe am I.[5]

Yes, we were once like Jonah. Now we pray, *Lord, make us less like Jonah, and more like Jesus.*

Looking Forward
Salvation Belongs to the Lord

The book of Jonah ends with the Lord's penetrating question to Jonah, "Should not I pity Nineveh?" and we might be left to wonder what happened to this enigma of a man, Jonah. But the fact that we have this book, his frank confession of his running and his resurrection and his resentment, is evidence that God was not done working in his life. In fact, in the very center of his book, because he wanted it to take center stage in his story, we find the settled conclusion of Jonah, the truth that reverberated through his life and experience, the truth that makes all the difference when it finds itself at the center of our lives.

Salvation belongs to the LORD! (Jonah 2:9)

Evidently Jonah wanted us to know that this book about him isn't really about him. It's about God, this one to whom salvation belongs. But what does that mean, and why does it matter?

Surely we could say that "Salvation belongs to the LORD" means that salvation begins and ends with the Lord. It is his work from start to finish. He is the one who initiates and accomplishes our salvation. He *has* saved us by putting our sin upon Christ and crediting Christ's righteousness to us. We are justified. He *is* saving us by sanctifying us by his Word and Spirit. And he *will* save us by glorifying us at the resurrection.

"Salvation belongs to the LORD" means that he chooses whom he will save. Oh, we must choose him, but our salvation is not solely a matter of our decision but of his choice. Aren't you glad to know that your salvation is not in your own hands, determined by your own ability to find him, understand him, trust in him, or change? Aren't you glad to know that your salvation comes through the sacrifice of another, the obedience of another? Praise God that salvation belongs to the Lord!

In the vision God gave to the apostle John, we discover that this profound truth reverberates into our current reality and on into the future. John saw a great multitude standing before the throne, "crying out with a loud voice, 'Salvation belongs to our God who sits on the throne, and to the Lamb!'" (Rev. 7:9–10).

There around the throne will be Jonah, perhaps surrounded by 120,000 people from the city of Nineveh. And he won't be angry, and he won't be sorry that God showed such great mercy to these, his brothers and sisters. All of his selfishness and bigotry will have been wiped away, and his heart will be full because the word of the Lord that came to him proved true—salvation belongs to the Lord.

Discussion Guide

Jonah

Getting the Discussion Going

1. Most of us have heard the story of Jonah taught before, and we might have taught it to children in Sunday school. As you think back, what are the usual lessons that have been taught from this story, and now what do you think is the main lesson we are intended to learn from the book? How might you title the story of Jonah?

Getting to the Heart of It

2. What did Jonah know about the Ninevites and about God that made him decide to defy God's instruction to go to Nineveh, and what did Jonah evidently not understand about God?

3. Talk through the scene on the ship in Jonah 1. What are some of the ironic and interesting things about it?

4. Who are the various people who repent in this story and what does their repentance look like?

5. Jonah's response to Nineveh's repentance and to God's relenting is not what most of us would like to record for posterity to read about us. Why do you think it was important to Jonah to include this in his book and to end his book this way?

6. What evidence would support the suggestion that "salvation belongs to the LORD" is the main message of the book of Jonah? Why is it good news that "salvation belongs to the LORD"?

7. Open to the page in your Personal Bible Study on which you wrote statements contrasting or comparing Jonah with one greater than Jonah, Jesus. Which of these was particularly significant to you?

Getting Personal

8. In what ways do you see yourself in Jonah and long to be more like Jesus and less like Jonah?

Getting How It Fits into the Big Picture

9. When we come to the New Testament, we see some of Jonah's attitude in assuming that God's mercy is just for the Jews. Read together the following verses and discuss how each expands upon the message of the book of Jonah: Matthew 28:18–20; Acts 10:34–43; 15:1–21.

Week 3

Hosea

Hosea

Hosea was a prophet to the northern kingdom of Israel, which he addresses by several different names in his book—Samaria, Jacob, and Ephraim. Each of these names emphasizes particular aspects of Israel's sins. Samaria was the center of idol worship, Jacob was known for his deceit, and Ephraim, the largest tribe in Israel, was the leader in rebellion.

1. In Hosea 1:1, Hosea lists those who were kings of Israel during the days when he prophesied. While this helps us to establish the time in which he prophesied, it also emphasizes the spiritual climate in which he ministered. Five of those seven kings are said to have continued in the sin of the first Jeroboam (2 Kings 14:24; 15:9, 18, 24, 28; 17:21–23). According to 1 Kings 12:26–29, what was this terrible sin that Jeroboam committed?

2. God's first message to his prophet Hosea must have been hard to hear and harder to obey. What did God tell him to do in Hosea 1:2 and why?

3. Read Hosea 1:3–9. Each of the names in this story is rich with meaning. The name Hosea means "savior," and he is presented in this story as a picture of Christ. The name Gomer, his wife, means "consumption," and she represents Israel, consumed by sin. What prophetic pronouncement is made by the names of each of Gomer's children?

Jezreel, which means "seed of God" or "scattered":

Lo-ruhamah, which means "no mercy":

Lo-ammi, which means "not my people":

4. As is typical in prophecy, the text throughout the book of Hosea moves back and forth between threatened judgment for continued disobedience and anticipated restoration as a result of repentance. What is the hope held out to God's people in Hosea 1:10–11?

5. Read Hosea 2:1–13 and listen to God speaking in poetic form through Hosea as an offended husband calling his unfaithful wife to repentance through threatened judgment. Note several words or phrases that indicate how Israel has offended the Lord.

Note several words or phrases that indicate what the Lord intends to do to Israel:

6. Once again, this oracle of judgment transitions quickly to an oracle of hope and restoration. Note several words or phrases from Hosea 2:14–23 that indicate what the Lord intends to do to restore Israel.

7. What will Israel do, according to Hosea 2:16?

8. In Hosea 3:1 the story of Hosea and Gomer picks up again with the Lord speaking to Hosea. What did God tell Hosea to do this time and why?

9. What did Hosea do, according to Hosea 3:2–3?

10. Just as Gomer was to purify herself by living with Hosea without giving herself to another man, what, according to Hosea 3:4, did Israel need to do to purify herself?

11. Hosea's pursuing, redeeming, and sanctifying love for Gomer provides us with a vivid and moving picture of Christ's love for us, his bride. Look up the following New Testament verses and write a sentence about Christ and his bride, the church, that corresponds to Hosea and his bride, Gomer.

Hosea and his bride, Gomer	Jesus and his bride, the church
Hosea took to himself a bride who was altogether unworthy of him, and totally without regard for him. (1:3)	Rom. 5:10; Eph. 2:12–13 *Christ took to himself a bride who was altogether unworthy of him and totally without regard for him.*
Hosea pledged his faithfulness to his bride, Gomer, not because he knew she would be faithful but knowing she would not be faithful. (1:2–3)	2 Tim. 2:13
Gomer's pursuit of other lovers brought her into bondage, slavery, and utter ruin. (3:2)	John 8:34; Rom. 6:20–23
Hosea redeemed Gomer by paying the ransom price of silver and barley. (3:2)	1 Cor. 6:20; 1 Pet. 1:18–19

Hosea redeemed Gomer, sanctifying her to himself. (3:3)	1 Thess. 5:23–25
Hosea loved his bride, Gomer, who was not pure, with the intention of making her pure. (3:3)	Eph. 5:25–27
Out of great love for Gomer, Hosea brought her home to live with him, where he could show kindness to her over the years to come. (3:3)	Eph. 2:4–7

12. Chapters 4–14 of Hosea are a cycle of oracles—covenant-lawsuit oracles that detail Israel's sin, judgment oracles that describe how God will deal with Israel's sin, and salvation or restoration oracles that describe what God will do to save his people from their sin.

    a. Note a word or two from the following verses that detail Israel's sin:

        4:1–2

        6:9

        7:7

        8:12

        9:10

        11:7

        12:1

        13:9

b. What are some of the consequences of Israel's infidelity found in the judgment oracles in these chapters?

4:6

5:9

7:11–12

8:14

9:12–14

10:15

c. Even though his people are unfaithful to him, the Lord has yoked himself to Israel and will not give up on them, just like Hosea did not give up on Gomer, even in the face of the rampant unfaithfulness. What does God promise to do to restore them?

6:1–3

8:10

11:10–11

14:4

14:5

13. As we read about God's promises of healing and restoration, we need to realize that while some of the promises may have been partially fulfilled when a small remnant of God's people returned to the land after the exile, all of these promises are ultimately and completely fulfilled in Christ. Hosea's prophecy presents God's loving commitment to preserve not solely Abraham's physical descendants but also his elect from every people and nation—Abraham's spiritual descendants, the Israel of God. Read the prophetic promise found in Hosea 1:10 and 3:5. How is it fulfilled, according to Romans 9:23–25; 11:25–26; and 1 Peter 2:10?

Teaching Chapter

Our Holy Husband

Before I was married, I had numerous people say to me, "When you find him, you'll know." I know they intended to be encouraging, but, honestly, I found it frustrating. Just *how* will I know? I wondered. Besides, I had my own trusted method of evaluating possible marriage candidates that is similar to how I prepare for a trip or plan my day: I made a list. On one side of the page I wrote out all the positives about a boyfriend, and on the other side I wrote out all the negatives. In every person and relationship, I was looking for the positive to significantly outweigh the negative. Surely that's how I will know, I thought.

My first date with David was on New Year's Eve, and when he left at about three in the morning, I have to admit to you, I knew. I don't think he knew quite so quickly. And certainly there was plenty more to learn about him, but there was that restful sense of being at home with him, of finding that he was just the right fit for me. It was only a few months later that I began wishing that he would ask me to marry him. And then one day I realized that I had not made the list. *What was I thinking? How could I be prepared to answer the question when and if it came if I had not made the list?* So one day, I sat down with notebook in hand, made my two columns on the page, and began to think it through. But I didn't get very far—not because there were no negatives or positives to list, but because I realized the question was not "Should I?" but rather "How could I *not* marry David?"

If we were going to make a list of what a woman needs in a husband, what would be on the list? We need to think this through, because, for the women who are reading this, whether we are married, widowed, divorced, never married, or separated—whether we are fulfilled in a happy marriage or lonely in a miserable marriage—we need a husband. It's not that the man we are married to or were once married to or hope to be married to or have given up being married to is not good enough. It's that we have needs that a human husband can never meet, no matter how good he is. If you are a man reading this book, you may be beginning to think that what I have to say is directed only to women. It isn't. The truth is, as strange as it sounds and as difficult as it is to grasp, perhaps even uncomfortable to consider, you, as a man, as a member of the bride of Christ, need the husband we're talking about in this chapter, too.

God has always spoken of himself as being a husband to his people. The prophet Isaiah wrote: "For your Maker is your husband, the Lord of hosts is his name" (Isa. 54:5). Through the prophet Jeremiah, God said, "I remember the devotion of your youth, your love as a bride, how you followed me in the wilderness" (Jer. 2:2). But it is the prophet Hosea who speaks of God as our husband in the most profound and even painful ways. Hosea was called to proclaim God's love for Israel as her husband, not simply in words but by making his life a living drama of God's unfailing love for his unfaithful bride.

If we were to make a list of what women really want and need in a husband, we find it here in the book of Hosea. In the first three chapters of Hosea we find a picture of our divine husband who chooses us, our husband who woos us to himself, our husband who loves us in the ways we need most to be loved.

> The word of the Lord that came to Hosea, the son of Beeri, in the days of Uzziah, Jotham, Ahaz, and Hezekiah, kings of Judah, and in the days of Jeroboam the son of Joash, king of Israel. (Hos. 1:1)

Here we have the historical setting in which this love story takes place. It is set in the middle of a nasty divorce, that between the tribes of Judah in the south and the tribes of Israel in the north, which had become two separate kingdoms. Hosea was a prophet to the tribes of Israel in the north, which did not have access to the temple in Jerusalem to worship the one true God but had ready access to and, in fact, were inundated by Canaanites and Canaanite altars.

Baal was the Canaanite god, a fertility god. The Canaanites all around them believed it was Baal who provided rain and fruitfulness and the harvest. So the Canaanites went to the "high places" and worshiped Baal by making offerings and having sexual relations with cult prostitutes, thinking that this would induce Baal to send rain and make the crops grow.

But what would make the people of Israel at all interested in Baal? They belonged to the one true God, the God who had given them a story, the God who had rescued them out of Egypt and brought them into the land and provided for them and blessed them. The Israelites should have known that their God was the only God, and they should have remembered how he had showered them with every good thing. We wonder how they could forget; yet we can also imagine how their worship of Baal might have gotten started.

Pastor Nigel Benyen provides a picture of how this might have occurred. He said that maybe one year the rains didn't come as early as they usually did, and they got a little anxious about the barley crop. Sitting on their front porch, perhaps they noticed a Canaanite neighbor heading off to the high places to worship Baal to try to get something going in the rain department. Later, when the neighbor came home and stopped for a chat with his Israelite neighbor over the back fence, he suggests that they go with him next time to increase the region's chances of rain. "Your God is wonderful, and it's wonderful what he did for you at the Red Sea if that really happened," he might say, "but it's not really that often that you need to walk through a sea on dry land, and we do need some rain right away. You don't have to give up worshiping your God; you're going to want to keep that up in case of a big emergency, but for day-to-day living, what you need is Baal." Then, after a few more days of no rain, the Israelite slips off with the neighbor to hedge his bets, adding a little Baal worship to his worship of the one true God. He has convinced himself that it's no big deal, when actually it is a great wickedness.[6]

God had made it clear since the beginning of his marriage to Israel that he would not share her with others. "You shall have no other gods before me," he had said (Ex. 20:3). But Israel persistently ignored his command. It was in this setting of widespread idolatry and forsaking the exclusive worship of the living God that God spoke to and through his prophet Hosea.

> When the LORD first spoke through Hosea, the LORD said to Hosea, "Go, take to yourself a wife of whoredom and have children of whoredom, for the land commits great whoredom by forsaking the LORD." (Hos. 1:2)

Wait a minute. Is this the Bible we're reading? This doesn't seem right. Surely God wants the prophet Hosea's marriage and family to be a good example to those around him and to us so that the people of his day would see what a pure marriage looks like and so we could read Hosea's story and find a message that is "safe for the whole family," perhaps offering us a guide for how to select a godly marriage partner, right? Evidently not. Evidently God intends for Hosea's bad marriage to be a living demonstration of his bad marriage to his people Israel. Evidently God's intention is for Israel to see herself in a story outside of herself so that she can see her worship of idols for the spiritual adultery it really is and come to repentance.

But most of us are a bit offended on Hosea's behalf when we read this request from God. We think, *How could God ask this of Hosea?* It seems cruel. What we must realize is that this story is in the Bible so that we will ask a completely different question, so that we will be offended on behalf of a different party. We're meant to ask, how could God put up with such repeated betrayal? We're meant to see that God is not cruel, but kind, not condemning, but merciful. This story is not about what God might ask you to do for him; it's about what he has done for you. We're meant to observe Hosea to see what our true husband's persevering love looks like in the face of *our* unfaithfulness. It is Gomer the prostitute, not Hosea the prophet, with whom we're meant to identify.

Now, I know you do not want to be labeled in such a degrading way, and I have no intention of labeling you this way. But I'm hoping you might be willing to open your heart to the message Hosea proclaims through his life and listen for what it might reveal about your own heart and ways. To see ourselves in this way does not come easily. We like to think that we are the good girls and the good guys. But we simply must lean in a little closer to this magnification mirror and face the truth about ourselves. There may be some things in our lives that we've thought are really not a big deal that are actually breaking the heart of God and need to be plucked out of our lives for good.

Do you find it hard to see yourself as one who has loved other gods? The things we idolize are not necessarily bad things. They are often *good* things that have become *ultimate* things. They are often legitimate desires that have morphed into destructive demands. Whatever we believe we *must* have for our happiness is an idol. We take something good—such as meaningful work—and turn it into an ultimate thing warped with ambition and greed. We take something good—such as parenting—and make it into an ultimate thing as we allow our identity to be defined by our child's success or failure. The question we have to ask ourselves is: Have I allowed something else, or someone else, anything else, to become the love of my life in the place that belongs to God alone? As we begin to get honest with ourselves about our true loves and passions, we're forced to admit that we can see ourselves in Gomer. And that would make us hopeless if we did not also see in her story our true husband. We have a divine husband who chooses us and takes us to himself in spite of ourselves. We see it pictured in Hosea's choosing and taking Gomer to himself.

He Chooses Us

> So he went and took Gomer, the daughter of Diblaim, and she conceived and bore him a son. And the LORD said to him, "Call his name Jezreel, for in just a little while I will punish the house of Jehu for the blood of Jezreel, and I will put an end to the kingdom of the house of Israel." (Hos. 1:3–5)

We don't know if Gomer was a prostitute before Hosea married her or if she became one later. Early on we do have some hope for this marriage, because she bore Hosea a son. But we also see that not only did the marriage deliver a message about God's relationship with his unfaithful people; the children born in this marriage, by their very names, also demonstrated and declared God's judgment on his unfaithful people.

By naming his son Jezreel, Hosea was reminding the people that he had not forgotten the bloody slaughter of the people in the town of Jezreel, perpetrated by King Jehu. It would seem that the very presence of this little boy declared the message that Israel would end up on the receiving end of such slaughter. (So Jezreel was probably not the kid in the neighborhood you wanted to invite over to play with your kids.) But he was not to be an only child. Gomer would bear three children, and each one would embody God's word to Israel.

She conceived again and bore a daughter. And the LORD said to him,

> "Call her name No Mercy, for I will no more have mercy on the house of Israel, to forgive them at all. But I will have mercy on the house of Judah, and I will save them by the LORD their God. I will not save them by bow or by sword or by war or by horses or by horsemen." When she had weaned No Mercy, she conceived and bore a son. And the LORD said, "Call his name Not My People, for you are not my people, and I am not your God." (Hos. 1:6–9)

Notice that the text doesn't say that Gomer bore these next two children, unlike the first son, to Hosea. Evidently Hosea was not the father of these two. Gomer had gone trolling for other lovers, and every day as Hosea changed those babies' diapers and put food in front of them, Gomer's whoring was rubbed in his face. The names of those two children sent a clear message about God's intentions toward Israel. He would have no mercy on them, while he would have mercy on their brothers and sisters down south in Judah. He would disown them. The Israelites found their identity in being the people of God, but God said through the name of this third child, "You are not my people, and I am not your God."

In Hosea 2 we begin another cycle of judgment oracles that serve as a warning, as well as oracles of hope for reconciliation. When we look at the text on the page, we can see that we've moved from narrative story to poetry. In the poetry of this chapter, we can hear two voices speaking in unison in regard to their wives. Hosea and God seem to speak with one voice about the faithlessness of their wives, Gomer and Israel, and the judgment they deserve.

> Plead with your mother, plead—
>   for she is not my wife,
>   and I am not her husband—
> that she put away her whoring from her face,
>   and her adultery from between her breasts;
> lest I strip her naked
>   and make her as in the day she was born,
> and make her like a wilderness,
>   and make her like a parched land,
>   and kill her with thirst. . . .
>
> Therefore I will hedge up her way with thorns,
>   and I will build a wall against her,
>   so that she cannot find her paths. . . .
>
> Now I will uncover her lewdness
>   in the sight of her lovers,
>   and no one shall rescue her out of my hand. (Hos. 2:2–3, 6, 10)

This was devastating, but what Israel rightly deserved because of her spiritual adultery. But while the messages of judgment throughout the prophets were shouts of warning, they were not irrevocable sentences. We saw that in Jonah too. Evidently, God had no intention of allowing his wife's unfaithfulness to have the last word in their relationship. He had chosen her and taken her to himself. Rather than destroy her, he was going to woo her back.

He Woos Us

Listen as this oracle of judgment shifts to an oracle of hope. Listen for all the things God, as Israel's loving husband, said he would do:

> Therefore, behold, I will allure her,
>   and bring her into the wilderness,
>   and speak tenderly to her.
> And there I will give her her vineyards
>   and make the Valley of Achor a door of hope.

And there she shall answer as in the days of her youth,
    as at the time when she came out of the land of Egypt.

And in that day, declares the LORD, you will call me "My Husband,"
and no longer will you call me "My Baal." For I will remove the names of the
Baals from her mouth, and they shall be remembered by name no more.
And I will make for them a covenant on that day with the beasts of the
field, the birds of the heavens, and the creeping things of the ground. And
I will abolish the bow, the sword, and war from the land, and I will make
you lie down in safety. And I will betroth you to me forever. I will betroth
you to me in righteousness and in justice, in steadfast love and in mercy. I
will betroth you to me in faithfulness. And you shall know the LORD.

And in that day I will answer, declares the LORD,
    I will answer the heavens,
    and they shall answer the earth,
and the earth shall answer the grain, the wine, and the oil,
    and they shall answer Jezreel,
    and I will sow her for myself in the land.
And I will have mercy on No Mercy,
    and I will say to Not My People, "You are my people";
    and he shall say, "You are my God." (Hos. 2:14–23)

I will allure her, *I will* bring her, *I will* speak tenderly to her, *I will* give
her, *I will* remove from her, *I will* betroth her to me in faithfulness—*He*
will do it.

Instead of giving us what we deserve for leaving him, our God woos
us to come back to him in repentance. Knowing full well that we are
unfaithful, he determines to betroth us to himself forever. He will not
only *be* to us righteousness and faithfulness and steadfast love; he will
impart these things to us. This is more than we would ever think to put
on our list for what we want in a husband. God's righteous, life-giving
ways are going to become our ways. He will accomplish our justifica-
tion, giving to us the free gift of his own righteousness. He will do the
work of reconciliation that will bring us peace.

My friend, hear the gospel according to Hosea: the success of your
marriage to this bridegroom is not dependent on *your* faithfulness but
on *his*. Your perfect purity is not what your groom demands. You need
not wear an off-white dress to this wedding. He will clothe you in the

whitest white. He will clothe you in *his* purity, and he will work in you to purify you through and through. He will renew your mind by his Word so that you will think differently about what is meaningful and beautiful and valuable and desirable. He will convict you when you begin to wander away from him so that you will hurry back into his arms, and he will keep your heart from becoming hard.

When we get to Hosea 2:23, it is as if God cannot wait to cancel out the appalling names given to Gomer's children of harlotry. Hosea practically sings in anticipation of grace as he declares God's intention: "I will have mercy on No Mercy, and I will say to Not My People, 'You are my people.'"

Oh, how thrilled and relieved we are to hear this! We hate to spoil it by asking any questions. But we must. We have to ask: How could God do this? On what basis could he seemingly overlook his bride's unfaithfulness? How could he be a truly good husband yet so unjust as to see this evil and simply let it go?

In fact, he would not let it go. In his perfect justice, punishment was to fall—but not on his bride. All the judgment described in the first half of Hosea 2 would be poured out in full on a substitute—his beloved Son.

∼ It is not those who reveled in their rebellious nakedness who would be stripped naked. God's own Son would be stripped naked and hung upon a cross.

∼ God would not make his unfaithful wife like a parched land and kill her with thirst, but rather his faithful Son would be parched and would cry out "I am thirsty" as he endured the unquenchable thirst that you and I deserve to feel forever.

∼ It is not Israel who would be hedged in with thorns, but his Son, who would have thorns pressed into his tender flesh.

∼ It is not the guilty wife left unrescued out of his hand of judgment but the innocent Son. Jesus drank the cup of judgment to the dregs. He received no mercy so that you and I could receive abundant mercy.

Are you not wooed by such love? Is your heart not broken by such sacrifice? Or somewhere along the way, has your heart become unbreakable so that you are no longer moved by the reality that the punishment you deserve was poured out on Christ, even as the blessing he deserves has been poured out on you?

The Lord is not done using Hosea's life and marriage to draw pictures for us. He has shown us how God chose us and took us in, how God woos us and binds himself to us in mercy, and in Hosea 3, we see how he loves us.

He Loves Us

Though Gomer had been tenderly loved by her husband, she refused to let herself be satisfied by him. She gave herself to all kinds of other lovers. Who knows how long she'd been gone when Hosea recounts:

> And the LORD said to me, "Go again, love a woman who is loved by another man and is an adulteress, even as the LORD loves the children of Israel, though they turn to other gods." (Hos. 3:1)

Notice that the Lord did not simply tell Hosea to go and get Gomer. He said, *"Go again, love a woman . . ."* The whole point is that Hosea was putting skin on the story of the Lord's love for his unfaithful wife. And just as God pursued his unfaithful wife, not in rage or retribution, so must Hosea.

I want you to imagine for a moment at this point in the story that you are Hosea's brother or sister. You've seen what has gone on over the course of years. You told Hosea not to marry her in the first place, but he didn't listen. You've helped with the kids and heard him weeping in his room after running into Gomer around town in the embrace of yet another man. You've watched Hosea grow old alone while he continues to long for Gomer to come home. And you've given him a piece of your mind more than once, telling him how she has made a fool of him. And then he tells you: "Gomer's latest lover has tired of her. He sees her simply as an aging prostitute, and he's willing to sell her back to me. So I'm headed down there to buy her back. I have only fifteen shekels in cash, so I'm taking some barley to make up the rest, and then I'll bring her home and we'll start over."

This is too much! How many times does she have to walk out before he finally has enough of her? She doesn't deserve this kindness! She'll prob-ably take advantage of him again! This simply makes no sense. Common sense says, "Enough!" But this is not common sense speaking; it's abundant grace. Hosea says simply, "I love her, and I want her back." And we read:

> So I bought her for fifteen shekels of silver and a homer and a lethech of barley. (Hos. 3:2)

"So I bought her." Do those words stir anything inside you? She belonged to Hosea. Long ago he chose her and bound himself to her. She was the one who had turned her back on his love and betrayed that love again and again. Once again, God is helping us to see that his covenant love is not based on *our behavior* but on *his promise.* Hosea did not commit himself to Gomer based on her past behavior or future potential but on his promise. And, my friend, God did not chose *you* and bind himself by covenant to *you* based on your past behavior or your future potential, but on his promise. This promise, a covenant commitment to love an unfaithful wife, comes with a cost. For Hosea it cost him the price of a common slave. But for God, the cost was the life of his own Son.

> You were ransomed from the futile ways inherited from your forefathers, not with perishable things such as silver or gold, but with the precious blood of Christ. (1 Pet. 1:18–19)

Can you see that this is what the love of God looks like—buying you back from the slave market and taking you into his home? There's more.

Hosea could have taken Gomer home and made her his personal slave at that point. He could have made her life miserable, reminding her of all her past whoring. He could have determined to make her feel all the hurt and humiliation he had experienced day after day for years. But he didn't.

> And I said to her, "You must dwell as mine for many days. You shall not play the whore, or belong to another man; so will I also be to you." (Hos. 3:3)

Hosea took her home to live with him, to be close to him. But there was some realism in his plan. Lots of old habits would have to be dealt with, lots of old affections would have to be altered, and lots of entrenched ways of thinking and feeling would need to be purified. Now that she was his again, he intended not only that he would have her in his home but also that she would have him in her heart, displacing all previous lovers. This would not happen in a miraculous instant but in a purifying process. He had sanctified her to himself by setting her apart from other men. And he would continue to sanctify her as that separation from other lovers and fidelity to him worked its way through her whole being.

Perhaps you know that God has redeemed you and set you apart for himself. *Do you sense he is now at work in you, washing away the dirty little habits and misery-producing patterns that defined your life before he redeemed you? Is he bringing healing to the scars on your emotions that drove to you other lovers? Is he replacing your enslaving addictions with newfound affections for him alone?* This is the way our holy husband loves us, which is why Paul instructed human husbands to love their wives in this way.

> Husbands, love your wives, as Christ loved the church and gave himself up for her, *that he might sanctify her, having cleansed her by the washing of water with the word,* so that he might present the church to himself in splendor, without spot or wrinkle or any such thing, that she might be holy and without blemish. (Eph. 5:25–27)

God has loved you. When you were not even looking for him, he chose you and determined to make you his own. He wooed you to himself with gospel promises of mercy instead of punishment, belonging instead of estrangement. He loved you by redeeming you from your enslavement to all lesser lovers, and he is loving you even now as he cuts away from your character every lingering tether to your old way of life. So the question really is not: *Does this God live up to your list of what you think you need most in a husband?* The question is, *Have you become united to this husband who knows exactly how you need to be loved? Or are you still playing the field, keeping your options open?* Hear his voice wooing you away from anything and everything that whispers false promises in your ear.

Perhaps your heart breaks in a special way when you hear this story because you have been married to a spouse who has gone after another lover. If that is the case, it is not at all hard for you to feel the broken heart that God wants us to feel when we read this story. You know exactly what it feels like. I'd like to challenge you in a couple of ways. First, would you allow your shared experience with the God of heaven to draw you into deeper intimacy with him? The betrayal and injurious rejection you've experienced allows you to have fellowship with God in a unique way because you share with him the broken heart of seeing the object of your affection in the arms of another lover.

The other way I want to challenge you is harder. You may have become trapped on top of a mountain of self-righteous resentment from which you have looked down on your unfaithful human spouse for a long time now. Though you identify with Hosea, perhaps you are beginning to see yourself in this story, not as innocent Hosea but as unfaithful Gomer, as one who has been unfaithful to your divine husband. Would you allow this recognition of your own unfaithfulness to your divine husband to begin to melt away the mountain of resentment you have toward your human spouse? Would you allow the mercy that you have been shown to overflow toward the one who has hurt you so deeply?

Perhaps this imagery of seeking satisfaction in the bed of someone other than your spouse is not simply a metaphor for idolatry but a reality in your experience. Earlier I said that an idol is anything apart from God that we feel we must have to be happy. So to disobey God's clear commands about reserving sexual intimacy for marriage is really a demonstration that we have said, "I do not trust that your laws are good for me, that you will provide for me in your timing. I must have this now to be happy." I will not lie to you and tell you that sexual patterns are easily changed or that the scars of sexual sin are instantly healed. You and I both know better than that. But there is healing held out to you. Jesus, the one who has paid the penalty for everything you've done, is the one who holds out this healing. He has no desire to punish you or shame you or condemn you. But he does insist that you stop crawling into bed with those you are not married to, even as he offers himself to you in a deep, personal way to empower you to change. He will take you back and will not shame you. Perhaps others around you or you yourself have written across your life, "No Mercy," or "Not my people." But I invite you to look again and see that Christ has written across your life in the red letters of his own blood: "Cleansed," "Forgiven," "Beloved," "Accepted," "Mine." And if this is what Christ says of you, *who are you to keep condemning yourself?*

Years ago I stood at the front of a church with my groom, David, and he said to me, "I, David, take you, Nancy, to be my wife, to have and to hold from this day forward." And he has held me for twenty-seven years now. In fact, I've always wanted to renew those vows on an anniversary. Somehow, years down the road, I think those promises would be even more precious to me than they were the first time, because now David knows me. Now he knows so much more about what it's going to cost him to love me.

I wonder, as you've seen our true husband, who has chosen us and wooed us and loved us—do you find you want to make a vow to *him*, or to renew your vow to *him*?

Do you promise to take him as your husband for better or worse, knowing that in the years to come on this earth there will be plenty of worse followed by an eternity of better and better and better? Say it out loud if you want to: *I do.*

Do you take him for richer or for poorer, knowing that while you are the poor one in this relationship, he intends to spend an eternity showering you with the riches of his grace? *I do.*

Do you take him in sickness and in health, knowing that you are the sick one in the relationship and that he has taken all your sin sickness on himself so that he might give to you his infinite health? *I do.*

Do you promise to love him and cherish him, not until death do you part but beyond the bounds of this life, confident that, as Paul writes in Romans 8:38–39, "neither death nor life, nor angels nor rulers, nor things present nor things to come, nor powers, nor height nor depth, nor anything else in all creation, will be able to separate [you] from the love of God in Christ Jesus our Lord"? *I do.*

Do you pledge to him your faithfulness, knowing that it will become reality only as you welcome his Spirit to work in you to generate the fruit of faithfulness? *I do*.

I have no authority vested in me to pronounce you "husband and wife" and would never presume to do so. It is the Holy Spirit who seals us and bears witness to our spirit that we belong to Christ. But I do have these words of promise from the lips of our glorious groom: "All that the Father gives me will come to me, and whoever comes to me I will never cast out" (John 6:37).

Looking Forward
The Perfect Marriage

There has been only one couple in the history of humanity who had a perfect marriage. Adam and Eve, prior to the fall, were "one flesh" (Gen. 2:24). They were "naked and were not ashamed" (v. 25). They enjoyed unhindered intimacy and peaceful compatibility with no selfish agendas or shameful secrets—until sin sent them hiding in shame, passing the blame, and feeling the pain of ongoing conflict.

Yet throughout the Bible God uses human marriage as a picture of the relationship he intends to share with his people, and as we've seen in Hosea, it is not a good marriage. While he is faithful, his bride is faithless. While his commitment to love his bride comes at great cost, his bride repeatedly shuns his claims on her affections. But throughout Hosea we find hope for this bad marriage—hope that one day it will have the perfection that Adam and Eve once enjoyed in the garden—in fact, even better than what they enjoyed in the garden.

The Lord speaks to his bride through Hosea, promising that he will allure her back to himself so that she will enjoy the thrill of young love (Hos. 2:14–15). He will cause her to forget all her other lovers so that she will cherish their exclusive relationship (vv. 16–17). He will solidify and secure their relationship so that nothing will ever come between them again (v. 18). In being joined to her, he is going to share with her his own righteousness, justice, steadfast love, mercy, and faithfulness (v. 19). She will be wholly his, and he will be her God (v. 23). He's going to love her and forgive her so that she will blossom and flourish in the abundance of his love and blessing. She will be everything she was meant to be, and more (14:4–7). And she will be beautiful (v. 6).

When we come to the New Testament, we discover that all these promises are coming true in the lives of those who are joined to Christ. Jesus spoke of his ministry as that of a bridegroom coming for his bride (Matt. 25:1–13; Mark 2:19–20). God is, even now, fulfilling the promises he made through Hosea. He has chosen us and drawn us to himself (Eph. 1:4; John 6:44). He has set us apart to himself and is working in us his righteousness, justice, love, mercy, and faithfulness (Phil. 1:10–11). But this marriage still isn't perfect. While we love him, we love many other things. We know him, but we know in part (1 Cor. 13:12). We have found our home in him, but we are still waiting for the day when he makes his home with us for good. Our union with him is real and true, but it is not yet all that God promised through Hosea.

But our wedding day will come. In this present age, the church is betrothed to Christ (2 Cor. 11:2), and it is only after the return of Christ that our marriage will be fully consummated. On that day, he who began a good work in us will have completed it (Phil. 1:6). Our bridegroom's purifying, sanctifying, beautifying work will be complete so that we will come "down out of heaven from God, prepared as a bride adorned for her husband" (Rev. 21:2), ready for the marriage supper of the Lamb (Rev. 19:6–10). We will be adorned with his holiness, purity, and perfection. We will be "a glorious church without a spot or wrinkle or any other blemish. . . . Holy and without fault" (Eph. 5:27 NLT). There, finally, we will hear a loud voice from the throne saying, "Behold, the dwelling place of God is with man. He will dwell with them, and they will be his people, and God himself will be with them as their God" (Rev. 21:3). We will finally enjoy the perfect marriage we've always longed for, made possible by our glorious groom.

Hosea

Getting the Discussion Going

1. Nancy talked about her list making in regard to what she wanted in a human husband. What are some aspects of Christ that make him a desirable divine husband?

Getting to the Heart of It

2. In the Personal Bible Study, you went through Hosea 4–14 and found specific sins that Israel had committed. What were some of them, and why would those particular sins break God's heart?

3. Why do you think God would ask his prophet Hosea to do something so difficult and painful? If you lived in his day and observed his life, what message do you think you would have gotten from observing his life and hearing his prophetical oracles?

4. What would it have meant to the Israelites in Hosea's day to hear that God will call them "Not My People" and "No Mercy"?

5. In Hosea 3:1–3 we see several aspects of the salvation we receive through Christ illustrated by Hosea's saving Gomer from slavery. How do we see: election, redemption, adoption, and sanctification?

6. The oracles in Hosea 4–14 go through cycles of detailing Israel's sins, predicting the judgment to come, and promising a future restoration. In the closing chapter, the Lord says to Israel, "I will heal their apostasy; I will love them freely, for my anger has turned from them" (v. 14). How would you explain why God would do this when his people clearly deserve the judgments described throughout the book? (See Rom. 3:21–26 for help.)

Getting Personal

7. As you think about your own faulty faithfulness in relation to Christ, what does it mean to you that he writes across your life in the red letters of his own blood: "Cleansed," "Forgiven," "Beloved," "Accepted," "Mine"?

Getting How It Fits into the Big Picture

8. Read through the Looking Forward section of this chapter. How does this help you to understand when and how all the promises of restoration and blessing described throughout Hosea are being kept and will be kept?

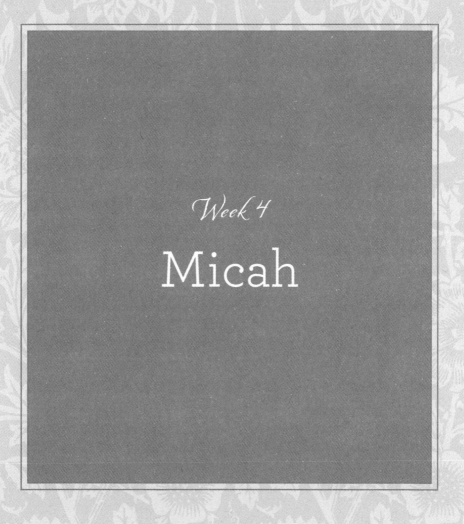

Week 4

Micah

Personal Bible Study

Micah

Micah 1:1 reveals where Micah was from, the kings who were on the throne over Judah when he prophesied, and who he was speaking to in his prophecy. While the prophecy concerns "Samaria and Jerusalem," meaning both the northern and southern kingdoms, we're going to see that Micah primarily used God's judgment against the northern kingdom, Samaria, through Assyria's invasion and imposed exile as a warning to the southern kingdom, Judah, encouraging them to repent so that they would not face the same fate.

1. When we read Micah, we need to recognize that it is not one letter or message. It is more like a collection of excerpts from Micah's prophetic oracles over the course of his seventy years of ministry. It can be divided into three sections. Note the similar way each section begins as well as the particular group being addressed in each section of his prophecy:

1:2

3:1

6:1–2

2. In Micah 1:2–9, Micah describes what is about to happen in the northern kingdom and eventually in the southern kingdom. What is going to happen and why?

3. Micah 2:1–5 describes those who lie awake at night thinking up ways to take land from their fellow Israelites (remember that land was allotted to families by Joshua when the Israelites entered the Promised Land). What key words describe these oppressors, and, according to verse 5, what will their judgment be?

4. According to Micah 2:6–11, what was the essence of the message the preachers in Micah's day were preaching?

5. In Micah 2:12–13, we have the first oracle of hope in the book. What does God promise in these verses?

6. According to Micah 3:1–4, though the civil leaders of Judah were responsible to execute justice, their cannibalistic exploitation of the poor and powerless revealed that they had no interest in walking in God's ways. What will their judgment be, according to 3:4?

7. In Micah 3:12–4:5, Micah predicts what will happen in Jerusalem in the near future and then in the latter days. What is it?

8. How was prophecy in Micah 3:12–4:5 fulfilled, according to the following verses?

John 2:19

John 12:32

9. In Micah 4:6–5:5 we discover that though the enemies of God's people are coming to destroy their cities, defile their temple, and humiliate their king, God is going to raise up for himself a king in Israel who will also be a shepherd. What are some details about this shepherd King, given in Micah 5:2–5?

10. How do we see this prophecy of a shepherd fulfilled in the following verses?

John 4:14

John 6:35

John 6:37

John 10:15

John 10:27

John 10:28

1 Peter 2:24–25

11. In Micah 6:6–7, Micah asks what God wants from sinners, escalating from less costly to more costly sacrifices. List the sacrifices Micah considers.

12. What does Micah say that God really wants, according to Micah 6:8?

13. In Micah 6:9–16, a sentence is passed on those who engage in deceitful business practices that take advantage of the poor and weak. What is it?

14. In Micah 7:14–17, Micah offers a prayer on behalf of his people. What does he ask God to do?

15. According to the following verses, how was Micah's prayer answered?

Matthew 7:29

John 6:27

John 20:30

Hebrews 2:14

Hebrews 13:20

16. In Micah 7:18–20, Micah wonders how God can pardon iniquity, pass over transgression, and no longer be angry toward the repentant remnant of his people. How do Romans 3:24–26 and 8:1–4 help us to understand how this is possible (even more clearly than Micah could have understood it)?

Teaching Chapter

Law and Order

"In the criminal justice system, the people are represented by two separate yet equally important groups: the police who investigate crime and the district attorneys who prosecute the offenders. These are their stories."[7]

Sound familiar? I can remember watching the very first episode of *Law & Order* in 1990, and in the years that followed we certainly watched our share of the show. In fact, aren't we are inundated with television shows about the criminal justice system—about criminals and cops, judges and juries, guilt and innocence? Perhaps that familiarity serves us well as we open the book of Micah, because here God is essentially bringing legal charges against his people. In Micah we find accusations and evidence, a verdict and a sentence, an advocate and a judge, a plea for mercy and an undeserved pardon.

Micah was the mouthpiece for the person pressing charges, the person against whom the crimes had been committed: God himself. Micah's book details the people's sins and the judgment their sins deserved, as well as the hope available to those who deserved this devastating judgment.

So let's imagine ourselves in the courtroom scene that is the book of Micah. Micah was like a prosecuting attorney. God sent him to register a complaint against Israel and Judah, to prosecute God's covenant lawsuit. We're going to discover that in God's courtroom, sinners are dealt with in one of two ways: with either deserved condemnation or undeserved grace. While God is a righteous judge who carries out deserved judgment, he is also a merciful Savior who gives undeserved grace and full forgiveness to those who turn toward him in repentance.

The Defendants

The book of Micah opens by calling all the peoples of the earth to listen to what God has to say.

> Hear, you peoples, all of you;
>   pay attention, O earth, and all that is in it,
> and let the Lord GOD be a witness against you,
>   the Lord from his holy temple.
> For behold, the LORD is coming out of his place,
>   and will come down and tread upon the high places of the earth.
> And the mountains will melt under him,
>   and the valleys will split open,
> like wax before the fire,
>   like waters poured down a steep place. (Mic. 1:2–4)

This is a frightening scenario: God leaving heaven to come down to earth to witness in the trial in such a powerfully destructive way that the mountains melt and the valleys split open. However, when the people of the ten tribes in the northern kingdom and the two tribes in the southern kingdom heard these words, they might have stifled a cheer rather than felt fear. There was nothing they wanted more than for God to come down and deal with all the people "out there" whom they saw as evil—the other nations who posed a constant threat to their security. But Micah continues:

> All this is for the transgression of Jacob
>   and for the sins of the house of Israel. (Mic. 1:5)

"Wait a minute," they must have said. "What do you mean that God is going to come down on *us*? We're not the evil ones. We're the ones who carry God's name in the world. Surely you don't mean that this disaster is going to come down on us!"

Oh, but that is exactly what God meant. The Assyrians were about to march into Israel and take the northern tribes into exile. Micah writes that "her wound is incurable," meaning that God's judgment on the northern tribes was inevitable, and that, sadly, "it has come to Judah; it has reached to the gate of my people, to Jerusalem" (1:9). Micah had hoped that the people of Judah, the southern kingdom, would see the destruction about to sweep over their northern brothers and sisters and would learn from their mistakes so that they would not face the same fate. But as he looked around Judah, he saw the same sins that he knew deserved the same judgment.

In 1:10–16, Micah worked his way through the towns in his beloved Judah that were about to be caught up in this disaster, including, in verse 14, his hometown, Moresheth-gath. His heart was broken as he saw in his mind the faces of people he knew and loved and anticipated their homes being burned and their families being separated, as the strong were taken off into captivity and the weak were left behind to fend for themselves. For Micah, this was not just some story about something happening in some far-off place and time. His heart was broken.

The Charges

Why was this about to happen? What had Israel and Judah done to deserve this kind of misery? In chapter 1 we see that when the Lord comes, he promises:

> All her carved images shall be beaten to pieces,
>   all her wages shall be burned with fire,
>   and all her idols I will lay waste. (Mic. 1:7)

The first charge is of rampant, pervasive, outrageous idolatry. The Ten Commandments begin with: "You shall have no other gods before me. You shall not make for yourself a carved image. . . . You shall not bow down to them or serve them" (Ex. 20:3–5). The defendants in Micah are the descendants of those who had promised, when given the Ten Commandments, "All the words that the LORD has spoken we will do" (Ex. 24:3). And here they were. They had put many other gods before Yahweh. They had erected household shrines to false gods and made regular trips to the temples of Baal. God charged them with breaking his law through their idolatry. In chapter 2 we find more charges:

> Woe to those who devise wickedness
>> and work evil on their beds!
> When the morning dawns, they perform it,
>> because it is in the power of their hand.
> They covet fields and seize them,
>> and houses, and take them away;
> they oppress a man and his house,
>> a man and his inheritance.
> Therefore thus says the LORD:
> behold, against this family I am devising disaster. (Mic. 2:1–3)

Here the charge is coveting, which had led to scheming and stealing. Micah paints a picture of aggressive, even violent oppression—powerful people lying awake at night making plans for how they will work the system to seize the property of vulnerable people. They were plotting ways to back less powerful people into a corner so that they would be able to take their land by force or pressure. They were figuring out which officials they could bribe to manipulate the legal system in their favor. Remember that when God's people came into the land of promise, Joshua apportioned it to tribes, clans, and families. Every family's inheritance of land was a physical, tangible benefit and sign of being God's covenant people. That's why the law God gave provided for ways in which people could get back their family's land if they lost it due to unpaid debts. God's people were always to have their allotment of God's land. However, in Micah's day that loving provision in God's law was being ignored.

So they were being charged with idolatry and covetousness and oppression. But there's more. In Micah 6, Micah asks:

> Shall I acquit the man with wicked scales
>> and with a bag of deceitful weights?
> Your rich men are full of violence;
>> your inhabitants speak lies,
>> and their tongue is deceitful in their mouth. (Mic. 6:11–12)

Their business practices were corrupt. They'd adjusted the scales down at the store so that people who thought they were buying a pound of wheat or barley were actually getting only 14 ounces. The businessmen were not living up to their contractual agreements. Lying, for them, had become a way of life. While they had agreed to obey commandments eight and nine, "You shall not steal. You shall not bear false witness against your neighbor" (Ex. 20:15–16), they were stealing with every business transaction, and nothing they said could be trusted.

Micah was showing us that God is interested in how we make our money. He's not so much interested in how much money we have, but he is interested in how we made it. We live in a culture of cutthroat competition and get-rich-quick schemes that often take advantage of weaker people in our society. So we need to ask ourselves, does the way I make money contribute to the community? Or do I make money by taking advantage of the misfortune or vulnerability of others? Micah calls us to open up our books and business practices to the scrutiny of a holy God, looking for how they line up with his heart for his people.

His heart for his people has always been that they would deal with each other with integrity. God had brought his people out of slavery in Egypt and into the Promised Land, intending that it would be an outpost of the goodness of heaven, a place of righteous justice, a place where the fatherless, the widow, and the sojourner would find refuge in a hostile world. God intended that the way his people would love him exclusively and live with each other righteously would put his glorious goodness on display for the world to see. But clearly that was not happening in Micah's day. And just as shocking as the people's rebellion against God's law was who they had as coconspirators.

The Coconspirators

Remember that Micah 1 began with the prophet speaking for God to all the peoples of the earth. In Micah 3, God zeros in on a specific group of people:

> Hear this, you heads of the house of Jacob
>   and rulers of the house of Israel,
> who detest justice
>   and make crooked all that is straight,

> who build Zion with blood
>   and Jerusalem with iniquity.
> Its heads give judgment for a bribe;
>   its priests teach for a price;
>   its prophets practice divination for money;
> yet they lean on the LORD and say,
>   "Is not the LORD in the midst of us?
>   No disaster shall come upon us." (Mic. 3:9–11)

These leaders were the very ones whom God's people were supposed to be able to go to when someone was stealing from them or threatening to take their land. But the leaders were taking bribes, so the powerless couldn't get any justice. The priests who were supposed to be teaching the law of God and calling the people to come clean before God were just telling people what they wanted to hear. And there were many prophets who, instead of listening to the Lord's voice, were calling on evil spirits to assist them in prophesying. Of course, what these false prophets told the people sounded nothing like what Micah or other faithful prophets such as Isaiah or Hosea were saying. While the true prophets warned of the destruction to come, the false prophets assured people that they did not need to worry their pretty little heads about that. They said, "Come on. We're the chosen ones. God gave us this land. He lives right up the hill in the temple. God would never let anything like that happen to us."

The Evidence

But the evidence was irrefutable and couldn't be ignored. Throughout his book, Micah laid it out. It wasn't hard to find; it was all right there in plain sight. We can almost see Micah standing at the center of the city, pointing to the evidence all around him. He would have pointed to the poles erected in front yards for worshiping the goddess Asherah. He would have held up the property deeds that the leaders conspired to wrest from families who lived on the wrong side of the tracks. He would have gestured to the long line at the fortune-teller's house and held up a set of dishonest scales from the local granary. The evidence was all there.

The Witnesses

If Micah were looking for witnesses to testify, there would have been plenty to choose from. There were prostitutes who lived at the temples to Baal and had kept records of the names and dates of all their liaisons. There were the homeless mothers with their children who had been driven off their land. The Lord, however, calls on the mountains to testify against his people:

> Hear what the LORD says:
> Arise, plead your case before the mountains,
>   and let the hills hear your voice.
> Hear, you mountains, the indictment of the LORD,
>   and you enduring foundations of the earth,
> for the LORD has an indictment against his people,
>   and he will contend with Israel. (Mic. 6:1–2)

The mountains had been there all along. They were witnesses to the covenant that God made with his people so long ago. They heard the thunderous voice of God giving his commandments at Mount Sinai, and they heard God's people pledge to obey. They were covenant witnesses.

One setting in which we have covenant witnesses in our common experience is a wedding. The true role and responsibility of those who stand beside the bride and groom at a wedding ceremony is to serve as witnesses to the covenant commitments made that day. When we say yes to being a bridesmaid or groomsman, we are not just committing to buying a dress or renting a tux; we are saying that we will be there to hold the bride and groom accountable to their vows. As covenant witnesses, there may come a day when we have to say, "I was standing there when you promised to love, cherish, honor, and keep your spouse. Is that what you are doing?"

The mountains were there when the Israelites made the promise to obey, and they've had a bird's-eye view to all the ways God's people have broken that promise. They've watched God's people make their treks to the high places to build altars to false gods. They have looked down on the city and seen the oppression of the weak. But the mountains are not the only witnesses called to testify. God himself sits in the witness box, saying:

> For I brought you up from the land of Egypt
>   and redeemed you from the house of slavery,
> and I sent before you Moses,
>   Aaron, and Miriam.
> O my people, remember what Balak king of Moab devised,
>   and what Balaam the son of Beor answered him,
> and what happened from Shittim to Gilgal,
>   that you may know the righteous acts of the LORD. (Mic. 6:4–5)

The Lord's testimony is not about what his people have done to him, but about what they seem to have forgotten. He redeemed them and led them and delivered them and protected them from enemies along the way. He forgave them and blessed them, but they have presumed upon him and ignored him and defied him.

The Defense

At this point in the proceedings, it is the defendants' turn to offer a defense, but the defense has nothing to offer. Instead, they suggest that God is simply impossible to please:

> With what shall I come before the LORD,
>   and bow myself before God on high?
> Shall I come before him with burnt offerings,
>   with calves a year old?
> Will the LORD be pleased with thousands of rams,
>   with ten thousands of rivers of oil?
> Shall I give my firstborn for my transgression,
>   the fruit of my body for the sin of my soul? (Mic. 6:6–7)

It's as if they are saying to God, "What do you want from me?" Offering sacrifices at the temple had clearly become an empty religious ritual, devoid of any true awareness of sin, let alone sorrow over it or repentance from it. Sacrifice had become a way to buy off one of their many gods.

So here in the prophecy, the defendants work their way through a series of mocking proposals to come up with a sacrifice that will satisfy

God, each one escalating in value. They begin with a calf and escalate not just to one ram but to thousands of rams; not just to a cup of oil but to a ridiculous ten thousand rivers of oil; not just to animal sacrifice but to the outrageous offering of a human sacrifice, a firstborn son.

Isn't this the way we deflect culpability for our failures to live by God's law—to suggest that what God requires from us is simply impossible, that the real problem is not our sin but an impossible-to-please God? Micah interrupts their attempt to deflect the blame by stating simply and clearly what the Lord does require from his people. And it isn't outrageous sacrifice; it is simple obedience from the heart:

> He has told you, O man, what is good;
>   and what does the LORD require of you
> but to do justice, and to love kindness,
>   and to walk humbly with your God? (Mic. 6:8)

Israel is supposed to offer sacrifices, but those sacrifices are supposed to be expressions of the sacrifice of a life lived in communion with God.

Hear the heart of God telling you, through his prophet, what really matters to him. It matters to him that you act justly—that you do what is right even when it is costly, that you refuse to take advantage of the vulnerable, that you become a person who, with increasing consistency, can be counted on to do what is true and right. It matters to God that you love kindness, or mercy. Notice that this is not just a call to be kind but to *love* kindness. This is kindness that flows out of a heart like God's heart.

Those who live with us have front-row seats to know whether this is true of us. When your spouse or a friend or a family member hurts or disappoints you, do your children see you simmer in resentment? Do they hear you rant about the offense to your friends over the phone? Or do they see that you actually love to show mercy in such situations? It matters to God that you walk humbly with him. There is a calm consistency to this, a "long obedience in the same direction."[8] To walk this way is to have the praise of God on our lips, a settled determination to be obedient to God in our hearts, and the evidence of God's transforming work on our character showing in our day-to-day lives. But it begs the question, how are we doing in regard to living this way? And if this is what the Lord requires, how will we ever meet his requirement?

While the people of Israel and Judah waited on the verdict, their leaders assured everyone that they had nothing to worry about. "We're God's people," they were saying. "Remember all of those promises he made to bless us?" Yes, God did make promises to bless his people if they obeyed. But these leaders were conveniently forgetting that he had also made promises to curse if they disobeyed. My friend, no one can persist in living a life of unrepentant idolatry, cruel oppression, and consuming covetousness, and presume upon the grace of God to save them in the end. That was a delusion then, and it is a delusion now.

The Verdict

The verdict is in. Other gods: guilty. Graven images: guilty. Taking the Lord's name in vain by calling themselves God's people while not living like they belonged to him: guilty. Forgetting the Sabbath: guilty. You see, the judge on the bench is not merely an objective onlooker. He is the one sinned against. Dishonoring father and mother: guilty. Murder: guilty. Adultery: guilty. Theft: guilty. False witness: guilty. Coveting: guilty. God's people were guilty of breaking every commandment.

The Sentence

And swiftly the sentence is passed.

> Therefore because of you
>   Zion shall be plowed as a field;
> Jerusalem shall become a heap of ruins,
>   and the mountain of the house a wooded height. (Mic. 3:12)

Micah was given eyes to see into the future, and he saw the Babylonian army crushing and cutting into the people of Judah like a plow cuts through dirt in a field. He saw the walls of Jerusalem reduced to a pile of rubble. He saw the temple in Jerusalem desecrated and stripped of its glory and beauty. It was a bleak sentence. Yet for those among the guilty who would come clean and confess, for those who would forsake their idols and change their wicked ways, there was hope:

> I will surely assemble all of you, O Jacob;
>   I will gather the remnant of Israel;
> I will set them together
>   like sheep in a fold,
> like a flock in its pasture,
>   a noisy multitude of men. (Mic. 2:12)

God promised that he would gather a remnant of his people from the land of their exile, a remnant made up of those who continued to love the God who had made such incredible promises to them and who continued to seek to obey his covenant from the heart. God would gather them like a shepherd gathers his sheep from the field and brings them into the safety of the fold. God would come as a shepherd. But that's not all. He would also come as a king:

> He who opens the breach goes up before them;
>   they break through and pass the gate,
>   going out by it.
> Their king passes on before them,
>   the LORD at their head. (Mic. 2:13)

As their king, God would break through every barrier to lead his people into his great city, where he will reign over them forever:

> I will make the remnant,
>   and those who were cast off, a strong nation;
> and the LORD will reign over them in Mount Zion
>   from this time forth and forevermore. (Mic. 4:7)

Micah had the distinguished honor among all the Old Testament prophets of predicting exactly where this shepherd King would come from:

> But you, O Bethlehem Ephrathah,
>   who are too little to be among the clans of Judah,
> from you shall come forth for me
>   one who is to be ruler in Israel,
> whose coming forth is from of old,
>   from ancient days. (Mic. 5:2)

This shepherd King would come from the little town of Bethlehem, just like his great-great-great-great-grandfather, David, who was also a shepherd King. His coming was still in the future, but in another sense, his "coming forth is from of old, from ancient days." The ruler who would come has existed into eternity past and will sit on the throne of David into eternity future. He would be the fulfillment of the ancient promise made to Adam of a descendant who would crush the head of the seed of the Serpent, and the fulfillment of the promise made to Abraham of a descendant through whom all the families of the earth will be blessed, and the fulfillment of the promise to David of a son who will sit on his throne forever:

> And he shall stand and shepherd his flock in the strength of the LORD,
>   in the majesty of the name of the LORD his God.
> And they shall dwell secure, for now he shall be great
>   to the ends of the earth. (Mic. 5:4)

This shepherd King would majestically rule over his people and shepherd his flock, which will one day extend beyond the borders of Judah to the ends of the earth. To the people who had spent their lives warding off threats yet were about to face the horrors of an invading army and foreign exile, Micah says of the shepherd King who would one day come:

> He shall be their peace. (Mic. 5:5)

Oh, how good this must have sounded to them. It is not just that the shepherd King would finally bring peace; he was to *be* their peace.

But how would this happen? This question takes us back to our courtroom scene. There we see the shepherd King standing with the defendants. He is their advocate before the great judge. The shepherd King has come not only to plead their case; he has come to take their punishment.

The judge has said, "They shall go . . . into exile" (Mic. 1:16). But the shepherd King says, "Send me into exile in their place so that they can draw near to you."

The judge has said, "Zion shall be plowed as a field; Jerusalem shall become a heap of ruins" (Mic. 3:12). But the advocate says: "Plow me as a field. Make me a heap of ruins so that they can be preserved by you."

The shepherd King says to the judge: "You said you would make Judah a desolation, its inhabitants a hissing, and that they shall bear scorn. But I come before you asking that you make me a desolation, a hissing. Let me bear the scorn they deserve. I will bear the indignation of the Lord. Pour out your anger on me, so that you can pour out your mercy on them. They have not done justice or loved kindness or walked humbly with you, but I have. Will you credit to them my perfect record of justice, mercy, and walking humbly with you? I will be their shepherd and will gather them into the safety of the fold. I will be their king and will rule over them in righteousness. I will be their peace" (see Mic. 6:16; 7:9).

At this point, the judge turns to those found guilty, those who have accused him of being impossible to please, and says, "You asked if I would be pleased for you to give your firstborn son for your transgression. I do not require the sacrifice of your firstborn. I will sacrifice my firstborn, so that you might go free." It's almost too much to bear, too good to believe. "God so loved the world, that he gave his only Son" (John 3:16).

Micah preached his message to the entire population of Israel. And the sad reality is that for the vast majority of those who heard Micah's preaching, it made no difference. Life went on the same. Another day, another dollar, still caught up in the same old sins. But there were a few—a few who realized that God was really speaking to them, a few who turned to God and repented. They asked for God's pardon and prayed for God's help to begin living a different kind of life. They heard what Micah said about the shepherd King, and they put their faith in him, not knowing when he would come or exactly who he would be but believing that he would come and save them by gathering them to himself as a shepherd and ruling over them and in them as their King.

This is the "remnant of his inheritance" that Micah speaks of as his book draws to a close (Mic. 7:18). To this remnant, the judge turns and says: "I will have compassion on you; I will tread your iniquities underfoot, I will cast all your sins into the depths of the sea" (see v. 19).

This is amazing not just for them but for us! While they looked forward in faith and put their confidence in the shepherd King and received this promise, we look back in faith and put all our confidence in this shepherd King, this one who is everything the Lord requires. He is at work in us by his Spirit, treading our iniquities underfoot through a sanctifying process, ridding us of our idolatry so that we no longer bow down to the false gods of financial success, physical beauty, and having the perfect family. The way we use and abuse the vulnerable around us, the way we crave the next new thing, all of our little white lies and shading the truth to get ahead—it is all being crushed underneath the feet of our almighty shepherd King.

At this point, Micah speaks for everyone observing what is taking place in the courtroom: "Who is a God like you, pardoning iniquity and passing over transgression for the remnant of his inheritance?" (Mic. 7:18).

In reality, we are all defendants in this courtroom. In this courtroom God is the judge, and our sins constitute the evidence against us. He has weighed the evidence, and we have been found guilty. The sentence has been passed: the wages of sin is death (Rom. 6:23). Our only hope is if someone else will take this sentence upon himself. And someone else has. If you have come into the safety of the fold of the shepherd and under the authority of the King, you can rest easy knowing that "the free gift of God is eternal life in Christ Jesus our Lord" and that "there is therefore now no condemnation for those who are in Christ Jesus" (Rom. 6:23; 8:1).

The good news of the gospel is this: *In the ultimate justice system, we are not represented by separate groups. The one who has investigated our crimes and the one who prosecutes offenders is also the one who pleads our case and absorbs our punishment. Our shepherd King is not concerned merely with law and order but also with grace and mercy.* This is our story. This is our confident hope.

Looking Forward

The Latter Days

There is a stark contrast between the end of Micah 3, where we read that Zion will be plowed as a field and Jerusalem will become a heap of ruins, and the beginning of Micah 4, where we read:

> It shall come to pass in the latter days
>   that the mountain of the house of the LORD
> shall be established as the highest of the mountains,
>   and it shall be lifted up above the hills;
> and peoples shall flow to it. (Mic. 4:1)

Here is a picture of glorious restoration, a picture of the temple being raised up from the rubble in such a way that it will draw people from every nation into its glory. Micah said this will happen in "the latter days," or as some translations put it, in "the last days." The term "latter days" was used not only by Micah but also by Isaiah (Isa. 2:2); Jeremiah (Jer. 23:20); Ezekiel (Ezek. 38:16); Daniel (Dan. 10:14); and Hosea (Hos. 3:5). So if we are going to understand what the prophets have to say about what is to come, we need to understand what they are referring to when they talk about the "latter days."

The Jews saw history broken up into two ages—what they called "this age" and "the age to come" or the "latter days." "This age" was the era captured in Old Testament history. "The age to come" was when the Messiah would bring their exile to an end and establish the kingdom of God over all the earth.

About a hundred years after Micah prophesied, a small group of God's people came back to Jerusalem and rebuilt the temple, to a degree. Yet the intensity and scope of the restoration Micah wrote about far surpasses the reality of their experience upon their return. Micah foresaw a day when God would come visibly and personally to his "mountain of the house of the LORD" in Jerusalem (Mic. 4:1).

The "latter days" began when God, in the person of Jesus Christ, stood on the mountain to "teach us his ways . . . that we may walk in his paths" (Mic. 4:2). In his death and resurrection Jesus brought the peace and abundance and security of which Micah spoke. When Jesus, the true temple, was lifted up from the earth, thereby drawing all men to himself (John 12:32), it was a fulfillment of Micah's prophecy that when the temple is lifted up, "peoples shall flow to it" (Mic. 4:1).

So when Jesus came two thousand years ago, we entered into "the latter days." That seems strange to us, because it seems so long ago. We've mistakenly understood the references in the Old and New Testaments about the "latter days" or "last days" to be exclusively about the time immediately prior to the second coming of Christ. What we fail to grasp is that the life, death, resurrection, and ascension of Christ is the center point of history and so ushered in the latter days. Ever since then, and until Christ comes again to set up the new heavens and the new earth, we are living in the "latter days," the final stage of human history. Even now we are experiencing the fulfillment of Micah's prophecy as, through faith in Christ, we are being taught his ways by his Word and enjoying the peace, abundance, and security found only through Christ.

But we have not yet experienced the fullness of Micah's prophecy concerning the latter days. The nations are not yet streaming to worship the God of Jacob as they one day will. Swords have not been beaten into plowshares or spears into pruning hooks (Mic. 4:3). Nation still lifts up sword against nation. The day has not yet come when all the peoples "walk in the name of the LORD our God forever and ever" (Mic. 4:5). But that day is coming. One day Christ will bring all things to their glorious end. The "last days" will culminate in the "last day" (John 11:24). And when that day comes, "the Lamb in the midst of the throne will be their shepherd" (Rev. 7:17). Our shepherd King will be on his throne, protecting, providing, and ruling over us forever and ever.

Discussion Guide

Micah

Getting the Discussion Going

1. The prophet Micah prophesied during a time in Israel and Judah that was marked by bribery, dishonesty, oppression, shameless idolatry, judicial corruption, and vain religiosity. And on top of all of this, the Assyrians, known for their cruelty to conquered lands, were an ever-present threat. Imagine if you had lived in Judah during this time. What might your life have been like?

Getting to the Heart of It

2. Micah was clear that God was about to judge the sin of Israel and Judah by using the Assyrian and Babylonians, who would take them into exile. But he was also clear that there was hope. What was the hope that Micah presented to God's people of his day?

3. Perhaps the most well-known verse of this book is Micah 6:8. Is this still what God requires of his people? What does it mean?

4. Micah promised that God would come as a shepherd, and in 7:14 Micah prayed for God to come and shepherd his people. How was this prophecy fulfilled and prayer answered?

5. Read Micah 7:18–20. What does this reveal about how God will deal with the sin of the "remnant of his inheritance"?

6. Micah, whose name means, "Who is like Yahweh?" concludes his book with the question, "Who is a God like you?" What about God is revealed in this book that leads to this rhetorical question?

Getting Personal

7. Jesus is presented to us in this book as our shepherd King. How have you or would you like to experience his shepherding care and his kingly rule?

Getting How It Fits into the Big Picture

8. Read through the Looking Forward section and then look back at Micah 4:1–7. How were various aspects of the verses fulfilled in the coming of Christ the first time, how are they fulfilled in the era in which we now live, and how will they be fulfilled when Christ comes again?

Week 5

Isaiah

Isaiah

1. Isaiah begins (1:1) by telling us about the kings who ruled over Judah during Isaiah's prophetic ministry. Note several things about each of these kings from the following passages:

Uzziah (2 Chron. 26:1–5, 16–23):

Jotham (2 Chronicles 27):

Ahaz (2 Chronicles 28):

Hezekiah (skim 2 Chronicles 29–30; 31:20–21; 32:22–26):

2. Isaiah 6 tells us about the vision Isaiah was given "in the year that King Uzziah died." Since Uzziah ruled for fifty-two years, he would have been the only king Isaiah had thus far known. With that in mind, why might Isaiah have needed to see the vision, recorded in Isaiah 6:1–7, at that time?

3. Read John 12:37–41. What does this reveal about who Isaiah saw on the throne?

4. Isaiah 9:2–7 speaks of a king who is going to come. "A child is born" speaks of the king's humanity, while "a son is given" speaks of his deity. What are the four titles given to this God-man king, and what does each reveal about what it will be like to live in his kingdom?

5. Isaiah 11:1–5 speaks of the reign of a greater David. Think about the kind of kings who sat on David's throne after David. What aspects of this greater David stand out as a welcome contrast to the kings who had ruled over them?

6. God's answer to the needs of his people is not just a king to rule over them but a servant to serve them. How will the servant serve God's people, according to the following passages?

42:1–7

49:1–6

50:4–9

52:13–53:12

7. In chapters 55–65 of Isaiah, we are introduced to the great conqueror. What do the following passages reveal about the person and work of the conqueror?

55:3–5 (understand that "him" in v. 4 refers to King David, and "you" in v. 5 refers to the conqueror)

61:1–3

63:1–6

8. Read Luke 4:16–21 and Revelation 19:11–21. What do these verses reveal about when the conqueror has or will fulfill the prophecies in Isaiah 61:1–3 and 63:1–6?

9. Throughout Isaiah's book we find the word "behold" repeated again and again. This is an instruction to look carefully, examine, take it all in. For each of the verses below, write a statement about what we are to "behold" and what it reveals about Christ?

Isaiah 6:7 with Hebrews 9:26 and 1 John 2:2:

Isaiah 17:4 with Matthew 1:20–23:

Isaiah 28:16 with Romans 9:33 and 1 Peter 2:6:

Isaiah 32:1 with Romans 14:17–18:

Isaiah 35:4 with 2 Thessalonians 1:7–9:

Isaiah 42:1 with Matthew 3:17; 12:18–20:

Isaiah 52:13 with John 3:14–15; 12:38–41:

Isaiah 62:11 with Matthew 21:5:

Isaiah 65:17 with 2 Peter 3:13 and Revelation 21:1:

Teaching Chapter

There Are Some Things You Can't Unsee

I noticed recently that one of the pastors at my church had a photograph of himself and one of the other pastors taped to his office door. The two of them were dressed up for some event in tank tops, athletic shorts, black kneesocks and dress shoes, with bandanas tied around their heads, standing back-to-back with their arms crossed and a look on their faces like they were going into battle. The pastor warned me not to look too closely at the picture. "There are some things you can't unsee," he said. And I suppose he was right. I can still see these two friends in my mind's eye, and it makes me smile. Life in this modern world includes being inundated on a daily basis with images from television programs, advertisements, websites, Facebook, and Youtube, some of which we just can't unsee. Some images stay forever engraved on our memories.

The prophet Isaiah had that experience. Isaiah was enabled by God to see some things that everyone else around him could not see, images that changed everything about the course of his life. The book of Isaiah is essentially a gallery of the images the prophet saw, expressed in words. The people of his day needed to see what Isaiah saw regarding the condition of their society and the hypocrisy of their religion. People who lived generations after Isaiah who found themselves in exile needed to see what Isaiah saw in order to believe that

God was not finished with them. And we too need to see what Isaiah saw. We need it to make a deep impression on us, because what Isaiah saw we never want to unsee.

In a world in which we are tempted to think that if only the right person would get elected to office, then everything would be okay, we need to see the ruler that Isaiah saw. In a world in which we are tempted to think that God is really lucky to have people like us in his corner, we need to see ourselves as Isaiah saw himself.

In a world enamored with gaining and wielding power, we need to see the servant whom Isaiah saw. In a world in which we simply must blog and tweet about our every experience and opinion, we need to see the one who did not open his mouth. In a world obsessed with physical beauty, shape, and form, we need to see the one who was marred and had no beauty that we would be attracted to him. In a world weighed down by shame, we need to see the one Isaiah saw who took our guilt upon himself.

As we live in a world where what God calls an "abomination" is held up as admirable, and a world in which his name is most often used as a thoughtless swear word, we need to see the warrior whom Isaiah saw who would come to put an end to all rebellion against his holiness. And as we live in a world in which babies die before they are born, and children go hungry in famines, and wars make women into widows, and cancer robs men of dignity, we need to see the future Isaiah saw in which there will be no more tears or pain.

If it is true that there are some things you can't unsee, surely this is something we need to see and never want to unsee.

The book of Isaiah begins by telling us what we are about to read:

> The vision of Isaiah the son of Amoz, which he saw concerning Judah and Jerusalem in the days of Uzziah, Jotham, Ahaz, and Hezekiah, kings of Judah. (Isa. 1:1)

We are going to read a collected record of the visions given to the prophet Isaiah over the course of his prophetic ministry, which spanned the reign of four different kings in the southern kingdom of Judah.

When Isaiah began his prophetic ministry, both the northern kingdom of Israel and the southern kingdom of Judah were experiencing a time of great political stability and comfort. Nevertheless, the world power at the time, Assyria, presented a real threat right outside their borders, and Isaiah saw a much bigger threat inside Judah's borders. Isaiah saw a sinful people who had forsaken the Lord in their hearts and lifestyles even as they went through the motions of religion, offering sacrifices at the temple. But fortunately he saw much more than the people's sins. He saw in the distant future someone who would save the people from the sins that defined them and the worldly powers of evil that threatened them. He saw a King who would reign in holiness. He saw a servant who would be everything Judah had failed to be. He saw a conqueror who would put an end to everything that had brought his people pain. Let's look, with Isaiah, for this divine King, this suffering servant, this coming conqueror.

Isaiah Saw a Divine King

> In the year that King Uzziah died I saw the Lord sitting upon a throne, high and lifted up; and the train of his robe filled the temple. (Isa. 6:1)

When we read, "In the year that King Uzziah died," it doesn't mean much to us. We don't live in a society in which kings—good or bad—hold the reigns of absolute power. Every few years, we witness a peaceful transfer of power from one elected official to the next. So we need to understand what it meant to the southern kingdom of Judah, and to Isaiah personally, that King Uzziah had died. It meant that there would be great anxiety about what the future would hold, based on what the next king would be like. Uzziah, the only king Isaiah had known at this point in his young life, was dead.

In the midst of this anxiety-ridden reality, the Lord enabled Isaiah to see that the real King was not dead. He was and is gloriously seated on the throne of the universe. It is this divine King, not the next human king, on whom Isaiah should pin his hopes. When Isaiah caught a glimpse of the real King, everything about his uncertain circumstances looked different. And when you and I, through the pages of Scripture, catch a glimpse of this real King, everything in our world full of uncertainties looks different. We realize we can rest secure. We don't have to be afraid of the future.

> Above him stood the seraphim. Each had six wings: with two wings he covered his face, and with two he covered his feet, and with two he flew. And one called to another and said:
>
> > "Holy, holy, holy is the LORD of hosts;
> > the whole earth is full of his glory!"
>
> And the foundations of the thresholds shook at the voice of him who called, and the house was filled with smoke. (Isa. 6:2–4)

The central truth impressed upon Isaiah about the real King is that he is holy. In fact he is more than that. He is holy, holy, holy—exponentially holy, separate from, other than, greater than, purer than, wiser than, more powerful than any king this world has ever known. And he is not just a king over one little stretch of land on the earth. "The whole earth is full of his glory!"

And what was Isaiah's response when he saw this glorious divine King? Did he dive in asking how God could allow his beloved Uzziah to die? Did he start working through his list of all the things he wanted this King to do for him? Did he begin pointing out the problems and the sins of the people all around him? No. He said, "Woe is me! For I am lost; for I am a man of unclean lips, and I dwell in the midst of a people of unclean lips; for my eyes have seen the King, the LORD of hosts!" (Isa. 6:5).

Isaiah was a prophet. His lips were poised to speak the very words of the God he loved. Yet when he saw the holiness of his God, he saw himself in a new light; he realized his lips were unclean. He recognized that what he really deserved was to be burned up in God's holy wrath. But instead of getting what he deserved, he was given what he did not deserve. That's grace.

> Then one of the seraphim flew to me, having in his hand a burning coal that he had taken with tongs from the altar. And he touched my mouth and said: "Behold, this has touched your lips; your guilt is taken away, and your sin atoned for." (Isa. 6:6–7)

In the Old Testament, fire stands for the unapproachable holiness of God, which both excludes and threatens (think burning bush, smoking Mount Sinai). But this glowing ember came to Isaiah's lips from the altar, the place where a sacrifice had been offered and accepted so that sin might be atoned for. This burning coal was "evidence that the fiery wrath of God had burnt itself out on the body of a substitutionary sacrifice."[9] This white-hot coal touched Isaiah's lips not to destroy but to cleanse.

Isaiah then offered his lips, his life, to speaking for God to his people. Of course, the message he was given by God, like the message of so many of the other prophets, was not what people wanted to hear. Isaiah's message was that their ongoing rebellion was going to result in exile. In Isaiah 6:11–13, Isaiah says that Judah was going to be mowed down by an invading army, like a buzz saw working its way through a forest until it is only a sea of stumps. But there is a glimmer of hope at the very end.

> The holy seed is its stump. (Isa. 6:13)

It is as if Isaiah could see a tender green leaf poking out of a pile of gray ashes in a field of burned stumps. Judah was going to be decimated but not obliterated. We gain more insight on this shoot emerging from the stump when we read:

> There shall come forth a shoot from the stump of Jesse,
>   and a branch from his roots shall bear fruit.
> And the Spirit of the LORD shall rest upon him,
>   the Spirit of wisdom and understanding,
>   the Spirit of counsel and might,
>   the Spirit of knowledge and the fear of the LORD. (Isa. 11:1–2)

This shoot was not just the reemerging nation of Israel but an individual, a person on whom the Spirit of the Lord would rest. Isaiah promised that a branch would shoot out of one of the trees mowed down in Judah—the family tree of Jesse, who was King David's father. At a time when the people of God were beginning to wonder how much longer a descendant of David would reign on the throne in Jerusalem, or if there would even be a throne in Jerusalem, Isaiah could see that God had not forgotten his promise to David of a throne on which one of his descendants would rule forever.

Isaiah saw a divine King, an accepted sacrifice, and a shoot from a stump. Who is this divine King whom Isaiah saw? In the Gospel of John, it is clear that Jesus is that divine King. Jesus said that he was going to be "lifted up from the earth," and John then quotes from Isaiah 6, writing, "Isaiah said these things because he saw his glory and spoke of him" (John 12:32, 41). Isaiah saw Jesus as he has always existed in the heavenly places before he became flesh. Sometimes we think that Jesus did not exist until he was born as a baby in Bethlehem. But for all ages before he became human, Jesus existed as God, with God, sharing God's glory in the throne room of heaven. Later in John's Gospel, we hear Jesus praying to his Father: "Glorify me in your own presence with the glory that I had with you before the world existed" (John 17:5). This was the glory Isaiah saw that day in the year that King Uzziah died.

What is this burning coal, this accepted sacrifice that provided cleansing instead of condemnation? It is the finished work of Christ on the cross applied to Isaiah in advance, when the burning coal touched his lips (Heb. 9:26; 1 John 2:2). What or who is this shoot, this fruitful branch emerging from the stump of Jesse? Who is this one on whom the Spirit of the Lord shall rest? Jesus, the Son of David, is the shoot from the stump of Jesse upon whom the Spirit descended in visible form at his baptism (Luke 3:23; Acts 13:22–23).

When Isaiah saw Jesus as the divine King, it put an end to his self-righteous pride. It put an end to his self-protecting anxiety. It put an end to his self-condemning woes. It filled him with Christ-exalting confidence that the divine King is on his throne, and this King will see to it that his purposes are accomplished. Oh, how you and I need to see this divine King! How we need a vision of this divine King to put an end to our pride, our anxieties, our self-condemnation. So we pray: *Open our eyes to see you, Jesus, in such a way that your royal glory can't be unseen.*

Isaiah Saw a Suffering Servant

Isaiah continues to speak to the sins of his people and the coming judgment of exile, but a huge shift takes place at chapter 40, as Isaiah moves away from addressing the political entanglements and spiritual failures of his day and begins to write for a future generation:

> Comfort, comfort my people, says your God.
> Speak tenderly to Jerusalem,
>   and cry to her
> that her warfare is ended,
>   that her iniquity is pardoned,
> that she has received from the LORD's hand
>   double for all her sins. (Isa. 40:1–2)

Why did God's people need to be comforted? Isaiah was writing this message—recording this vision—for a generation not yet born who was to experience the enormous discomfort of exile in Babylon. They would be tempted to think that God's plans for and promises to his people were a thing of the past. So God prepared words of comfort in advance that they would find on the scrolls of Isaiah, which their parents would take with them from Jerusalem. Isaiah's words would encourage them not to give in to despair. A couple of chapters later, Isaiah draws a portrait of an individual who will be the source of their comfort.

> Behold my servant, whom I uphold,
>   my chosen, in whom my soul delights. (Isa. 42:1)

Throughout the book of Isaiah, the Lord says to us again and again, "Behold!" It's as if he is saying, "Look at this! Here is something you have to see, something you must consider carefully." What is it the Lord wants us to look at so closely? He says, "Behold my servant."

A servant is a person who gets his master's will done. God is introducing the person who will get his will done in the world. He is telling us how his ancient promise to Abraham, to bless all of the families of the earth, is going to be delivered. Then he tells us how his servant would go about accomplishing what his master wanted done:

> He will not cry aloud or lift up his voice,
>   or make it heard in the street;
> a bruised reed he will not break,
>   and a faintly burning wick he will not quench;
>   he will faithfully bring forth justice.

> He will not grow faint or be discouraged
>   till he has established justice in the earth;
>   and the coastlands wait for his law. (Isa. 42:2–4)

His servant would not be a loud self-promoter. In a world full of broken reeds and smoldering wicks—people who have been injured by life in this broken world and are just hanging on—the Lord's servant will gently touch those in need of healing grace. But don't mistake his quiet compassion for weakness. This servant has the strength needed to punish wrongdoers and set things right—not just in a corner of the world but throughout the earth—and he will use it.

So who is this servant? If we look back in Isaiah 41:8, we find that Isaiah described his people, Israel, as "my servant." But we can't help but wonder if Israel was up to this task or even interested in it. In Isaiah 42:18–25, Isaiah answers that question with a resounding no. In these verses he points out that Israel was blind to God's glory (v. 18), spiritually insensitive (v. 20), and so bound up in disobedience that there was no way she could provide direction to anyone else (v. 22). Clearly the nation of Israel was not able to fulfill its calling to be God's servant.

When we come to chapter 49, we discover there was to be an individual who would be the servant God was looking for to accomplish his mission in the world. We get to hear the servant himself speaking. He says:

> The LORD called me from the womb,
>   from the body of my mother he named my name.
> He made my mouth like a sharp sword;
>   in the shadow of his hand he hid me;
> he made me a polished arrow;
>   in his quiver he hid me away.
> And he said to me, "You are my servant,
>   Israel, in whom I will be glorified. . . .
>
> "It is too light a thing that you should be my servant
>   to raise up the tribes of Jacob
>   and to bring back the preserved of Israel;
> I will make you as a light for the nations,
>   that my salvation may reach to the end of the earth."
>   (Isa. 49:1–3, 6)

This servant is the true Israel, who would be everything the nation of Israel was unable to be. How is it that this servant could bring salvation not just to sinful Israel but also to the ends of the earth? As Isaiah begins to answer that question, it is as if he could hardly believe the answer he was about to give. He writes: "Who has believed what he has heard from us?" (Isa. 53:1). The way the servant would go about this saving work would be quite stunning, not at all what we might expect.

Isaiah 52:13–53:12 is a hymn about this servant and how he will save. It is made up of five stanzas. The hymn begins by once again inviting us to "behold" the servant, and it allows us to "behold" the servant from several angles: as the world sees him, as God sees him, and as those who put their faith in him see him.[10]

In Isaiah 53:2–3 and 7–9, we see the servant as the world sees him. And clearly the world sees him with contempt. It is as if he is so offensive that they would rather not look.

> He had no form or majesty that we should look at him,
>   and no beauty that we should desire him.
> He was despised and rejected by men;
>   a man of sorrows, and acquainted with grief;
> and as one from whom men hide their faces
>   he was despised, and we esteemed him not. (Isa. 53:2–3)

When the world looks at the servant, it sees a tragic figure—innocent but too weak to speak up for himself:

> He was oppressed, and he was afflicted,
>   yet he opened not his mouth;
> like a lamb that is led to the slaughter,
>   and like a sheep that before its shearers is silent,
>   so he opened not his mouth.
> By oppression and judgment he was taken away. . . .
> although he had done no violence,
>   and there was no deceit in his mouth. (Isa. 53:7–9)

To the world, the servant is just another example of man's inhumanity to man. His life and his suffering is a waste. But that is just what the world sees. Isaiah also wants us to see the servant as God sees him.

While the world sees the servant's death as a great humiliation, God sees it as his great exaltation, as the hymn begins: "Behold, my servant shall act wisely; he shall be high and lifted up, and shall be exalted" (Isa. 52:13). Where the world sees only agony and defeat, God sees glorious victory: "I will divide him a portion with the many, and he shall divide the spoil with the strong" (Isa. 53:12). Most significantly, while the world sees the servant's suffering as useless and senseless, a tragedy at the hands of men, God sees the servant's suffering as purposeful, something he himself has done. "Yet it was the will of the LORD to crush him; he has put him to grief" (Isa. 53:10). God says that through the death of "the righteous one, my servant," many will be "accounted righteous, and he shall bear their iniquities" (Isa. 53:11).

We've seen how the world sees the servant and how God sees the servant. Next we see how those saved by the servant see him. Remember that faithful Jews who slayed a lamb every year at Passover did so believing that God accepted the blood of the lamb as a substitute to make atonement for their sin. Yet deep down they knew that an animal's blood could never truly atone for human rebellion. As the righteous servant came into focus, they realized *he* is the substitute that all the lambs throughout the years had anticipated. In the heart of the hymn we hear those saved by the servant say:

> Surely he has borne our griefs
>   and carried our sorrows;
> yet we esteemed him stricken,
>   smitten by God, and afflicted.
> But he was pierced for our transgressions;
>   he was crushed for our iniquities;
> upon him was the chastisement that brought us peace,
>   and with his wounds we are healed.
> All we like sheep have gone astray;
>   we have turned—every one—to his own way;
> and the LORD has laid on him
>   the iniquity of us all. (Isa. 53:4–6)

Centuries after Isaiah wrote those words, an Ethiopian royal servant traveled to Jerusalem to worship Yahweh in the temple. On his way home he was reading what Isaiah had written about the servant many centuries earlier. Acts 8 tells us:

> The eunuch said to Philip, "About whom, I ask you, does the prophet say this, about himself or about someone else?" Then Philip opened his mouth, and beginning with this Scripture he told him the good news about Jesus. (vv. 34–35)

Jesus is the servant who suffered as our substitute. Isaiah is taking our faces in his hands and pointing us to look at Jesus hanging upon the cross in our place. You may have seen a lot of amazing things in your lifetime but nothing is as important as seeing him there, not just as an innocent victim, a tragic figure, or a religious icon, but as the one who bore *your* griefs and was pierced for *your* transgressions.

Isaiah Saw a Coming Conqueror

In chapters 56–65 Isaiah looks further forward into the future of the people of God, to the time after the divine King condescended to live among his people and then ascended to his throne, after the servant's suffering has given way to glory. With Isaiah as our guide, we stand on tip-toe to see the future coming of the servant King, this time as a conqueror, who says:

> The Spirit of the Lord GOD is upon me,
>   because the LORD has anointed me
> to bring good news to the poor;
>   he has sent me to bind up the brokenhearted,
> to proclaim liberty to the captives,
>   and the opening of the prison to those who are bound;
> to proclaim the year of the LORD's favor,
>   and the day of vengeance of our God;
>   to comfort all who mourn. (Isa. 61:1–2)

If this passage sounds familiar to you, it's because Jesus stood up and read it in the synagogue in his hometown about a year into his ministry. Or, more accurately, we should say that he read part of it. He read up to the part about proclaiming the year of the Lord's favor. At that point:

He rolled up the scroll and gave it back to the attendant and sat down.
And the eyes of all in the synagogue were fixed on him. And he began
to say to them, "Today this Scripture has been fulfilled in your hearing."
(Luke 4:20–21)

Jesus stopped short of saying that he had come to proclaim "the
day of vengeance of our God; to comfort all who mourn." That's because
that day is still to come. Jesus came the first time to proclaim the Lord's
favor, which he showers now on all who repent and believe. When he
comes again, he will bring in the day of God's vengeance—a day all of
those who refuse to repent and believe have every reason to dread. As
we continue, Isaiah draws a picture of this coming day, this day of vengeance. And, frankly, it is a disturbing scene.

In the preceding chapters, Isaiah looked and longed for God to
come and rescue his people from the brokenness and madness of the
world. And when we get to chapter 63, suddenly, off in the distance, he
sees someone coming and asks:

Who is this who comes from Edom,
    in crimsoned garments from Bozrah,
he who is splendid in his apparel, marching in the greatness of his
        strength? (Isa. 63:1)

The Edomites were ancient and constant enemies of God's people.
While the Israelites were the descendants of Jacob, the Edomites were
the descendants of Esau. Throughout the Bible, Edom represents man
in his rebellion against God and his antagonism toward God's people.
Isaiah sees a lone warrior coming up from Edom, his clothes spat-
tered with red, and he asks who it is. And the warrior, marching in his
direction, replies, "It is I, speaking in righteousness, mighty to save"
(Isa. 63:1).

So Isaiah asks:

Why is your apparel red,
    and your garments like his who treads in the winepress?
        (Isa. 63:2)

And the conqueror answers:

> I have trodden the winepress alone,
> > and from the peoples no one was with me;
> I trod them in my anger
> > and trampled them in my wrath;
> their lifeblood spattered on my garments,
> > and stained all my apparel.
> For the day of vengeance was in my heart,
> > and my year of redemption had come. (Isa. 63:3–4)

That's blood on his clothes—the blood of those who have hated God and persecuted his people, the blood of those who have refused the offer of his blood to cleanse and renew them. This is the same vision, the same conqueror the apostle John saw in his vision many centuries later, which he wrote about in Revelation 19: "He is clothed in a robe dipped in blood, and the name by which he is called is The Word of God. . . . He will tread the winepress of the fury of the wrath of God the Almighty. On his robe and on his thigh he has a name written: King of kings and Lord of lords" (Rev. 19:13–16).

As unpleasant as it is to look at, we must. Knowing that God will execute righteous vengeance enables us to entrust our desires for vengeance to him. It gives us confidence that evil will not go unpunished. Justice will be done. Wrongs will be righted. Purging the world of evil is what will make the purity of the new heavens and the new earth possible, which the conqueror also wants us to see:

> For behold, I create new heavens
> > and a new earth,
> and the former things shall not be remembered
> > or come into mind. (Isa. 65:17)

Evidently, in that day when we enter into the new heavens and the new earth, the things we would really like to be able to *unsee*—the misery and cruelty we have witnessed, the way things have worked in a world under a curse—will be wiped away from our memories, never to be seen again. But until then, we want to behold our divine King reigning on his throne, the servant who suffered in our place, the conqueror who is coming to purge this world of evil. He is someone we never want to unsee.

Turn your eyes upon Jesus.
Look full in His wonderful face.
And the things of earth will grow strangely dim.
In the light of His glory and grace.[11]

Looking Forward

Glory Revealed

Glory is to God what brightness is to the sun or wetness is to water. It is his essential property that flows out of who he is. So whenever God reveals himself, it is his glory we see. And there are many ways in which we see his glory. The heavens display the glory of God. In some sense, everything God made reveals his glory.

God also revealed himself in a unique way in the Old Testament through the Shekinah glory. This was a physical manifestation of the divine glory of God that appeared to the Israelites of Moses's day as a pillar of light by night and a pillar of cloud by day. This visual expression of the divine presence of God was a perpetual reminder of God's commitment and care for them, even as they wandered for forty years in the desert because of their disobedience. But evidently the Shekinah glory on display in the wilderness or hovering over the temple in Jerusalem was not the full extent to which God intended to put his glory on display. Isaiah writes:

> And the glory of the LORD shall be revealed,
>> and all flesh shall see it together,
>> for the mouth of the LORD has spoken. (Isa. 40:5)

Isaiah pointed to a greater disclosure, a fuller revelation of God's glory in the future. Luke tells us about a fuller revelation of God's glory, which was put on display the night Jesus was born:

> An angel of the Lord appeared to them, and the glory of the Lord shone around them, and they were filled with great fear. (Luke 2:9)

Later, three of the disciples were given a special glimpse of the intrinsic glory of God in the person of Christ when they went up on a mountain and he was transfigured before them. John testifies about that experience, saying, "We have seen his glory, glory as of the only Son from the Father, full of grace and truth" (John 1:14). The fullness of God was seen as it had never been seen before in the person of Jesus Christ—in his life, death, resurrection, and ascension.

Though Christ has ascended, God's glory is even now being revealed. Paul tells us that the glory of the Lord is being revealed *in us* as the Holy Spirit transforms us into the image of Christ:

> And we all, with unveiled face, beholding the glory of the Lord, are being transformed into the same image from one degree of glory to another. (2 Cor. 3:18)

But surely Isaiah's promise of God's glory being revealed will find its full consummation when Jesus comes a second time. It is not until then that "all flesh shall see it together." Revelation says that in the new city, in which we dwell with him, there will be "no need of sun or moon to shine on it, for the glory of God gives it light, and its lamp is the Lamb" (Rev. 21:23). In the New Jerusalem, the glory of God will shine in its full strength. We won't need to shield our eyes from it as we will have new capacities for beholding it. In fact, the joy of heaven will be beholding the glory of God for all eternity.

Discussion Guide

Isaiah

Getting the Discussion Going

1. Most of us have memories or actual photographs of an event or a person that we can't unsee—something or someone that shaped who we are and the path our life has taken. What something have you seen that you will never unsee?

Getting to the Heart of It

2. In the Personal Bible Study, you were asked why Isaiah might have needed to see this vision of Christ as the divine King. Why do you think he needed to see it, and what difference do you think it makes for us to see it through the pages of Scripture?

3. How does Isaiah's God-given vision of Christ on the throne of the universe (Isaiah 6) differ from some of the stories we hear from people today who claim to have had a supernatural or died-and-came-back-to-life experience of seeing Jesus? How does Isaiah's response to this very real vision of Christ differ from the response of modern-day people who claim to have seen him?

4. In the hymn about the servant in Isaiah 52:13–53:12, Isaiah asks, "Who has believed what he has heard from us?" (53:1). Looking over the passage as a whole, what aspects of it would the people of Isaiah's day, and the people of our day, find difficult to believe?

5. The people who lived between the time Isaiah wrote his prophecy and the first coming of Christ anticipated the coming of the divine King and the suffering servant Isaiah wrote about, but they didn't anticipate that he would be one and the same person. How did Jesus demonstrate in his first coming that he is both the divine King and the suffering servant?

6. This picture of Jesus coming again as a conqueror and doing the work of destroying his enemies is uncomfortable for us. In fact, many today want to rid our understanding and proclamation of the gospel of this offensive imagery and reality. Why is it important that we not do that?

Getting Personal

7. Isaiah called us to turn our gaze toward Christ as the divine King, suffering servant, and coming conqueror. In which of these ways do you think you most need to see and refuse to unsee Christ today, and why?

Getting How It Fits into the Big Picture

8. Like so much of Old Testament prophecy, aspects of Isaiah's prophecy were fulfilled in his day, some soon thereafter, and some at the time of Christ, while some is yet to be fulfilled. For each of those categories, what examples from Isaiah can you think of?

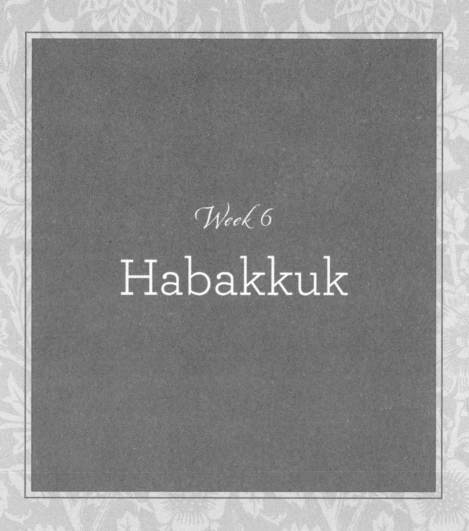

Week 6

Habakkuk

Personal Bible Study

Habakkuk

While most of the Prophetic Books are made up of oracles or messages given to a prophet to declare to God's people, in the book of Habakkuk we get to listen in on Habakkuk's personal back-and-forth with God (in the first two chapters) and his song to God (in the third chapter). To understand the things Habakkuk is talking to God about, we must know that he was a prophet in Judah, the southern kingdom, after the northern kingdom had been taken into exile by the Assyrians but before the southern kingdom was taken into exile by the Babylonians. Sadly, the people of Judah have not learned from watching their northern brothers and sisters be taken off into exile and have continued in their rebellion against God's law.

1. Read Habakkuk 1:1–4. What is Habakkuk's question or complaint regarding the situation in Judah in his day?

2. Read Habakkuk 1:5–12. In the Lord's answer to Habakkuk's complaint, Habakkuk discovers that God is doing something about Judah's evil. What is it?

3. Read Habakkuk 1:13–2:1. Habakkuk recognizes that God has ordained to use Babylon to bring judgment upon Judah. How would you summarize Habakkuk's problem with God's plan, expressed in verse 13?

4. In Habakkuk 2:1–3 what does Habakkuk determine to do, and how does the Lord respond?

5. As is typical in Hebrew literature, we find the key point of the book at the very center, in Habakkuk 2:4. God is about to tell how and why the wicked are going to perish under his judgment. What is the contrast to the reality that God presents in this verse?

6. This key phrase in Habakkuk (2:4) summarizes the path of life God sets out for his people and is quoted three times in the New Testament, highlighting a different aspect of its meaning each time. Read each of the New Testament passages that quote Habakkuk 2:4 and describe what you think is being communicated.

Romans 1:16–17

Galatians 3:11–14

Hebrews 10:38

7. In Habakkuk 2:6–19 the Lord pronounces a series of "woes" on the wicked, describing what their wicked ways will lead to. Try to put into your own words the wickedness that is addressed in each woe as well as what those who practice that wickedness can expect.

2:6–8: Woe to him who . . .

2:9–11: Woe to him who . . .

2:12–13: Woe to him who . . .

2:15–17: Woe to him who . . .

2:18–19: Woe to him who . . .

8. In the midst of these woes, Habakkuk is also a prophet of hope. What hope is found in verses 14 and 20?

9. The third chapter of Habakkuk is really a song, as indicated by "according to Shigionoth," in verse 1, which likely indicates the tune or tone of the song, and the notation at the end, "with stringed instruments" (v. 19). Read Habakkuk 3:1–15 in which Habakkuk recalls and celebrates God's actions in the past to rescue Israel, focusing especially on his saving acts when he brought Israel out of Egypt. Notice that sal-

vation for God's people is accomplished through judgment on God's enemies. How might recalling God's past salvation through judgment be helpful to Habakkuk and those he ministered to in his day?

10. The final section of Habakkuk's song (3:17–19) is the declaration of a righteous person who is resolved to live by faith. Understand that since Habakkuk lived in an agrarian society, the fig tree not blossoming, the olive crop failing, and the cattle dying represent a total loss of livelihood and a way of life. Try your hand and your heart in expressing your resolve to trust and rejoice in God, despite whatever may happen in the future, following Habakkuk's pattern in verses 17–19. You might begin by thinking through your greatest fears and what it would look like to trust God even if those fears become reality.

Teaching Chapter

Feeling Pretty Good about Myself

I think I have figured out the attraction of reality TV. It all became clear to me when I saw a post on Facebook the other day that said, "I absolutely love watching Hoarders. It makes me feel so much better about my own house." While I'm not a regular watcher of this show, which goes into the homes and the heads of people who collect so much stuff that they can't even move from room to room, I must admit that I've watched an episode or two and discovered it does have appeal. Somehow, when you see piles of junk in other people's homes, it can't help but make you feel better about that one little junk drawer in your kitchen.

As I thought about it, I realized that is really what all reality television does—it makes us feel better about ourselves. Watching people lie and scheme to win a million dollars makes us feel morally superior, quite sure that we would never lower ourselves to that level. In fact, if you want to feel good about your parenting, just watch an episode of any reality TV show that takes you inside the day-to-day life of a family. If you want to feel better about your singing, watch the auditions on the singing competition. And if you want to feel good about yourself in pretty much every way, just tune in to an episode of a *Real Housewives from Anywhere*.

I feel better about myself just thinking about the people on these shows, don't you? Or maybe you feel better about yourself right now because you never watch these shows!

In the book of Habakkuk, we meet the prophet Habakkuk, and he is in great distress about his people, Judah, the southern kingdom. It has been a while since their cousins in the northern kingdom of Israel were carried off into exile by the Assyrians, a direct result of rebelling against God. Habakkuk had hoped that the southern kingdom would have learned from the northern kingdom's mistakes. But evidently, when the people in the southern kingdom tuned in to what had taken place in the northern kingdom, they just felt better about themselves. Perhaps they said to each other, "Well, at least we aren't as bad as they were. At least we still have a descendant of King David's on the throne. At least we still go to the Jerusalem temple to worship." When they looked at their lives in light of their northern cousins, they felt pretty good about themselves.

But Habakkuk did not compare his people and their ways to how people around them lived. He looked at his people in light of God's law, God's holiness, and all God intended for his people to be. Habakkuk was sick about the state of God's people. Everywhere he looked, he saw people who should have known better doing very bad things. He saw people desperately in need of God to do something if things were to turn around. And Habakkuk couldn't see that God was doing anything at all.

Bad People and Their Need for God

Habakkuk got up every morning and read the *Jerusalem Daily News*. Every day he read about judges taking bribes to rule in the favor of the rich, murderers and rapists getting away with their crimes, and neighbors suing one another over land deals gone bad. And this was not happening somewhere outside the borders of Judah. It was happening among the people God had called to himself to be separate from the world, people to whom God had given his law so that they could live together in his land, enjoying his provision and presence, demonstrating to the world around them how good their God is. So Habakkuk took his question, which was really a complaint, to God himself.

> O Lord, how long shall I cry for help,
>   and you will not hear?
> Or cry to you "Violence!"

> and you will not save?
> Why do you make me see iniquity,
>   and why do you idly look at wrong?
> Destruction and violence are before me;
>   strife and contention arise.
> So the law is paralyzed,
>   and justice never goes forth.
> For the wicked surround the righteous;
>   so justice goes forth perverted. (Hab. 1:2–4)

Evidently Habakkuk had spent plenty of time on his knees begging God to do something among his people that would open their eyes to their evil and cause them to turn away from it and toward God's loving law. But as far as Habakkuk could see, God was doing nothing to bring new-ness to their life with him and their love for him. He wondered the same thing we wonder at times, such as when we have begged God to bring someone we love to him, or back to him, and God doesn't seem to be doing anything. He wondered, *God, do you even care?*

Really Bad People and the Holiness of God

In Habakkuk 1:5–11 we hear the Lord's answer to Habakkuk's heart-sick inquiry, which begins this way:

> Look among the nations, and see;
>   wonder and be astounded.
> For I am doing a work in your days
>   that you would not believe if told.
> For behold, I am raising up the Chaldeans,
>   that bitter and hasty nation,
> who march through the breadth of the earth,
>   to seize dwellings not their own. (Hab. 1:5–6)

God responded to Habakkuk's complaint, that he was seemingly doing nothing about wrong, by telling Habakkuk that he was, in fact, at work. He was doing something so stunning that Habakkuk wouldn't believe it. And when Habakkuk found out what it was, he didn't want to believe it. When Habakkuk heard God say, "I am raising up the Chaldeans," he thought that surely he had heard wrong. Habakkuk could picture in his mind what was about to happen as the arrogant armies of Babylon swept into Judah to devour it, laughing at all the misery they inflicted along the way. Perhaps at that point Habakkuk wanted to take back all his begging of God to do something. Clearly the treatment for his people's sin would be worse than the disease. *How could God use the most wicked people in the world against his covenant people?* It just didn't seem right to Habakkuk, so he said to God:

> You who are of purer eyes than to see evil
> and cannot look at wrong,
> why do you idly look at traitors
> and remain silent when the wicked swallows up
> the man more righteous than he? (Hab. 1:13)

Habakkuk remembered the story he had seen on *60 Minutes* about the Chaldeans, the world's most vicious fighting force from southern Babylon, which made him feel much better about his own people by comparison. He had been complaining about the wickedness of his own people, but in his mind they were "more righteous" than those evil Chaldeans. "We're bad," he thought, "but *we're not that bad. We're certainly not as bad as they are!*"

Habakkuk knew that God is pure and holy and cannot look at wrong. What he didn't understand was how, at the same time, it could be true that God would use a wicked nation as a tool to work his holy purposes amongst a "more righteous" (or, really, less wicked) people, the people of Judah. That just didn't seem right to Habakkuk. And we get that, don't we? Don't we wonder, at times, how God can allow an evil person, organization, or company to sweep into our lives and take away our home, our health, or our reputation? Perhaps we have been praying for God to work in our lives to make us more dependent on him, hungrier for his Word, more faithful in prayer. But certainly this is not the road we would have chosen to get us there. We wonder how God could use something or someone we see as evil as his tool to do a purifying work in our lives when we are so, well, so much more righteous than they are.

Yet when we look at Scripture, we see that God repeatedly used wicked people to accomplish his salvation purposes. Think of Joseph's brothers who cruelly sold Joseph into slavery. Later Joseph said to them, "As for you, you meant evil against me, but God meant it for good, to bring it about that many people should be kept alive, as they are today" (Gen. 50:20). Think of Israel's demand for a king, which God saw as a rejection of himself. Samuel told the people that their wickedness was great in demanding a king (1 Sam. 12:17). Yet God was at work through it to establish the throne on which the Son of David would one day sit.

Most significantly, look at the wicked people God used in the death of his Son. In Acts 4 we read what Peter prayed in Jerusalem shortly after Pentecost, a prayer in which he said to God, "For truly in this city there were gathered together against your holy servant Jesus, whom you anointed, both Herod and Pontius Pilate, along with the Gentiles and the peoples of Israel, to do whatever your hand and your plan had predestined to take place" (Acts 4:27–28). Peter, along with the other apostles, had come to see that God used the twisted hypocrisy and murderous plotting of the religious leaders, the deceitful betrayal of Judas, the self-centered demands of the people, the cowardly capitulation of Pilate, and the wicked wiles of Satan himself, to accomplish his purifying, restoring, saving plan for his people through the death of Christ. This wasn't a compromise of God's holiness but rather a demonstration of it. God, in his sovereignty, is able to use wicked people, wicked actions, wicked organizations, and wicked intentions to accomplish his good intentions in the lives of his people.

Of course, Habakkuk didn't have the whole of the Old and New Testaments to see this as we do. God's plan made no sense to him. Habakkuk had laid out his complaint against God, and he waited to hear God's answer. Then God spoke to Habakkuk:

> Write the vision;
> > make it plain on tablets,
> > so he may run who reads it. (Hab. 2:2)

God made clear from the get-go that his answer was not a private exchange between himself and Habakkuk; Habakkuk was to write it down so that it would be available to all the people of his day. But beyond those people, he was to write it down for the generations to come who would have some of the same questions Habakkuk had. God's answer to Habakkuk was written down for you and me because we too have wondered why God seems slow to act when we've begged him to intervene in our unjust circumstances. We too have struggled to make sense of how a good God can use evil intentions to accomplish his good purposes.

As Habakkuk stood poised and ready to write down God's answer, once again it was probably not what he had expected to hear. He wanted God to explain himself, but God held up a mirror to Habakkuk and his people so that they could see the reality of their souls:

> Behold, his soul is puffed up; it is not upright within him,
>   but the righteous shall live by his faith. (Hab. 2:4)

Somehow, in his upset about God's intention to use the wicked nation of Babylon, Habakkuk had lost sight of just how wicked his own people had become. Evidently he had become blind to the pride that had made itself at home even in his own soul, so that it had become "puffed up," "not upright." Habakkuk needed to hear that his claim of being "more righteous" was not going to exempt him and the rest of Judah from experiencing the judgment they deserved. God is not interested in puffed-up, better-than-the-next-guy righteousness. The truth is, anything less than perfect righteousness will not cut it with God. (How are you doin' with that?)

God was challenging Habakkuk, and us, not to depend on our own goodness if we're hoping to avoid his judgment. We cannot live just by trying to be better than other people. God does not lower his standards. He requires perfect righteousness. But what God requires, he also provides. God provides for those who put their faith in him, in the righteousness of another.

The Only Good Person and the Requirement of God

Habakkuk came to understand that he would be foolish to plead with God on the basis of his own righteousness or the relative righteousness of the people of Judah. Instead, if they wanted to live, they had to rely fully on the perfect righteousness of another, provided wholly by

God himself. What Habakkuk and the bad people of Judah needed, and what the really bad people of Babylon needed, and what bad people like you and me need, is the righteousness of the only truly and perfectly good person who has ever lived credited to our account.

Of course, Habakkuk couldn't see this righteous person as clearly as we can. But that didn't keep him from putting his faith in him. It would be another six hundred years before the source of the righteousness that became Habakkuk's by faith would be revealed. He witnessed to it by inspiration of the Holy Spirit, but he didn't know when this righteous one would come or exactly who he would be (1 Pet. 1:10–12). It was more than six hundred years later when Paul wrote, "But *now* the righteousness of God apart from the law is revealed, being witnessed by the Law and the Prophets, even the righteousness of God, through faith in Jesus Christ, to all and on all who believe" (Rom. 3:21–22 NKJV). Prophets such as Habakkuk witnessed to the righteousness of God in the person of Jesus Christ, long before he was revealed to the world.

So now we know who the "righteous" are. They are not the not-so-bad people. They are bad people who have received mercy—unrighteous people who have been declared righteous because they have taken hold by faith of the righteousness of Christ. They are unrighteous people who are being transformed into the image of the righteous one. But let's go back to this key verse in the book of Habakkuk, which tells us that the righteous "will live by his faith." What does that mean?

Living by Faith in the Promises of God

The remainder of the book of Habakkuk shows us at least five things about what it means to live by faith.

First, it presents the contrast to living by faith. We discover in the verses that follow what is going to happen to the wicked. While those who receive the righteousness of Christ by faith are going to live, those who have rejected the righteousness of Christ are going to perish in their sin. So the first lesson from Habakkuk in what it means to live by faith is that *living by faith means not perishing in your sin.*

God began painting the picture of the contrast between living by faith and perishing in sin in Habakkuk 2:6 with the word "woe." In fact, he didn't just say one "woe"; he said it five times. There are five woes directed at the really bad people of Babylon. If you want to understand what this series of woe statements really means, think of them as being the exact opposite of the "Blessed are you" statements found in the Beatitudes, which speak of the happy lives that those who humbly rely upon God and walk in his ways can expect in the future. Here in Habakkuk, the woes speak of the miserable death that will come to those who arrogantly reject God and his ways. God was making clear to Habakkuk that even though he intended to use the wicked Babylonians for his good purposes toward his people, he was not blessing the Babylonians. They would not escape the judgment they deserved.

"Woe to him who heaps up what is not his own," God begins (Hab. 2:6). God tells those who have abused power in order to accumulate wealth that they will find themselves abused and end up with nothing.

"Woe to him who gets evil gain for his house, to set his nest on high to be safe from the reach of harm!" (v. 9). God tells those who take advantage of others, who use their fortune to build mansions behind gates where they can't be touched by the ills of the society they helped to create through their exploitation, that the stones in the walls of their houses are going to testify against them at the judgment.

"Woe to him who builds a town with blood" (v. 12). God tells those who count human life of little value, those who thoughtlessly use people to create their own comfort, that everything they have collected will be been taken from them, and their comfort will be gone for good.

"Woe to him who makes his neighbors drink—you . . . make them drunk, in order to gaze at their nakedness" (v. 15). God tells those who keep filling up others' drinks, hoping inhibitions will be lowered and clothes will start coming off, and the seducer, the rapist, the pornographer, and those who think that looking at pornography does no harm, that they are going to end up exposed and ashamed.

"Woe to him who says to a wooden thing, 'Awake'; to a silent stone, Arise!" (v. 19). God tells those who worship the business they've built, the lifestyle they've guarded, the body they've chiseled, the reputation they've honed, that they will find death, not life, in those things.

God tells Habakkuk, and he's telling you and me, that he is going to deal with evil. It's all going to be brought to nothing. So the second thing we learn from Habakkuk about what it means to live by faith is that *living by faith means believing that justice will be done.*

As Habakkuk 3 opens, we sense that something has shifted in the prophet. He has witnessed the grace of God at work, providing an alien righteousness to undeserving people, promising life instead of death. And he has witnessed his holy God's intention not just to use wickedness for his purposes but to one day destroy wickedness for his glory. It is as if Habakkuk has left the courtroom where he had been interrogating God and gone directly to the temple to worship God. Chapter 3 is a song, a symphony of the soul. And Habakkuk invites us to sing along with him. Try to imagine how the opening verse of his song might have sounded as Habakkuk was thinking about the wrath of God that would come down on Babylon in the future. In song, he welcomed God to demonstrate his justice in wrath:

> O LORD, I have heard the report of you,
>   and your work, O LORD, do I fear.
> In the midst of the years revive it;
>   in the midst of the years make it known;
>   in wrath remember mercy. (Hab. 3:2)

The "report" he refers to is the record of God's dealings with his people in the past as recorded in the books of Moses. Habakkuk's song rehearses the history of a previous time when God used a wicked people—the Egyptians, who enslaved the Israelites—to bring about his redemptive purposes. Remembering how God came to fight for his enslaved people against the Egyptian army, using pestilence and plague and finally drowning them in the waters of the Red Sea, filled Habakkuk with confidence that God would again come to the aid of his exiled people and accomplish a second exodus. He asks God to do it again.

Rather than continuing to argue with God, he welcomes God to work. But he does have a request: "In wrath remember mercy." He's saying, "God, in all this upheaval and destruction, show mercy to the people on whom you've set your love. In the tumult of what is about to unfold, even though we rightly deserve to be caught up in the catastrophe, save us from complete annihilation." So the third thing Habakkuk reveals to us is that *living by faith means expecting that mercy will be shown.*

Evidently the Spirit of Christ enabled the prophet Habakkuk to see in his mind's eye how this prayer would be answered in the future, as a small remnant of those taken away from Judah would continue to live by faith far away in Babylon, and eventually return home. But beyond that, Habakkuk saw further into the future. He saw a greater salvation that would be accomplished when the wrath of God would be poured out not on an entire nation but on one man.

Habakkuk writes of him: "You went out for the salvation of your people. . . . You crushed the head of the house of the wicked" (Hab. 3:13). Ever since the garden of Eden, when God promised that the seed of the woman would one day crush the head of the seed of the Serpent, putting an end to his evil power, God's people had waited and watched for this descendant to come. Through the inspiration of the Holy Spirit, Habakkuk was writing about the day when the head of the house of the wicked, Satan himself, would be crushed by the seed of the woman, Jesus Christ, in his death and resurrection.

At the cross, God did come down in wrath. But he remembered mercy. Through the cross, mercy is extended to all who will, by faith, take the righteousness of Christ as their own, even as he took their sin as his own. So Habakkuk looked forward by faith, not only to the eventual short-term salvation God would work among his people by bringing them out of the land of Babylon and back home to Jerusalem, but to the greater salvation God would accomplish for his people through the work of his Son.

Habakkuk could see it, and he savored it. But he was a real person living at a particular time, so he also recognized that he and those he loved were going to have to endure some very dark days before the future salvation became a reality. Evidently, having eyes of faith regarding a future salvation didn't take away all his fear about what would happen in the in-between time. And we get that, don't we? When we read in these next verses that he was afraid of what life would hold in the near future, we get it, because though we believe

God's promises about a future salvation from difficulties, our belief doesn't always have the power to take away all our fear about today and tomorrow.

> I hear, and my body trembles;
>   my lips quiver at the sound;
> rottenness enters into my bones;
>   my legs tremble beneath me.
> *Yet I will quietly wait* for the day of trouble
>   to come upon people who invade us. (Hab. 3:16)

Habakkuk was saying, "I'm scared. I know there is heartache and loss ahead for me and for people I love, and there is a part of me that is really afraid as I think about the Babylonian invaders showing up on our doorstep. But I refuse to let this fear control me. I refuse to allow this difficulty in my short-term future rob me of my long-term hope. Because I believe that God will prove true to his promises to save his people and destroy his enemies, I can wait quietly. God has given me a glimpse of the day when the earth will be filled with the knowledge of the glory of the Lord as the waters cover the sea. And what I know to be true about this future glory and my own future sharing in it is actually changing how I feel about, and how I intend to face, this present pain."

Habakkuk was expressing far more than a fear-management strategy. This was not optimistic denial about the coming disaster. He was not pouring himself into praying away the coming disaster. He was entrusting his life and perhaps his untimely death to God. He chose to live by faith—not the kind of faith that believed God would miraculously show up and shield him from harm, but faith that God would preserve him and those he loved *through* harm. He was showing us the fourth aspect, that *living by faith means enduring whatever may come.*

Habakkuk has been giving us a song to sing, and at this point the feel of the song changes from a confession of very real fear to a declaration of just as real confidence:

> Though the fig tree should not blossom,
>   nor fruit be on the vines,
> the produce of the olive fail

> and the fields yield no food,
> the flock be cut off from the fold
>   and there be no herd in the stalls,
> *yet I will rejoice* in the LORD;
>   I will take joy in the God of my salvation. (Hab. 3:17–18)

Habakkuk shows us that living by faith means banking our hope on God, no matter what happens in this life. He discovered the door to a joy that was not dependent upon his circumstances; he trusted that God was in control of both the process and the outcome. Habukkuk's rugged trust reminds us of Job, who said in the midst of devastation:

> And after my skin has been thus destroyed,
>   yet in my flesh I shall see God. (Job 19:26)

It reminds us of David's determination not to fear in the face of death:

> Even though I walk through the valley of the shadow of death,
>   I will fear no evil,
> for you are with me;
>   your rod and your staff,
>   they comfort me. (Ps. 23:4)

Habakkuk's confidence in the glory to come after suffering reminds us of Paul's confidence in what was to come after his suffering:

> We do not lose heart. Though our outer self is wasting away, our inner self is being renewed day by day. For this light momentary affliction is preparing for us an eternal weight of glory beyond all comparison. (2 Cor. 4:16–17)

All these passages are teaching us to say to ourselves and to God: *In spite of the very real fear I feel, I know that I have nothing to ultimately fear. In spite of loss, I can be happy, confident that all that I need is mine in Christ.* That's living by faith. And there's one more thing Habakkuk shows us: *living by faith means trusting that God will get you safely home.*

> GOD, the Lord, is my strength;
>   he makes my feet like the deer's;
>   he makes me tread on my high places. (Hab. 3:19)

Habakkuk was confident that the Lord would enable him to navigate difficult situations. God would make him "tread on my high places," which is a picture of triumph over every threat to his living by faith. This triumph is the result of trust. As Habakkuk leaves us, he declares in the closing words of his song that he will persevere in spite of difficulty, confident that no matter the danger, nothing could ultimately harm him. He was safe and secure because his God is strong enough to preserve him even through death; his God keeps his promises to save.

I want that kind of faith, don't you? But how does that happen? Is this kind of faith in the face of disaster only for certain personality types? Is it really only for the super-spiritual among us? Is this one of those "fake it till you make it" things?

Hebrews is a book about faith. Near the end of it, the writer works his way through a list of people who lived by faith, people such as Abraham and Noah and Moses, whose lives testify to what it means to live by faith. Yet while the writer of Hebrews wants us to glance at the people who lived by faith, it is only on our way to setting our gaze firmly on the only person who ever perfectly lived by faith. He is telling us how you and I can live with radiant confidence in God, despite our circumstances.

> [Look] to Jesus, the founder and perfecter of our faith, who for the joy that was set before him endured the cross, despising the shame, and is seated at the right hand of the throne of God. Consider him who endured from sinners such hostility against himself, so that you may not grow weary or fainthearted. (Heb. 12:2–3)

If you and I spend our days looking around at other people, perhaps we will feel better about ourselves. If we stay focused on the difficulty of our circumstances, we'll always be living in fear instead of living by faith. But looking to Jesus puts everything else and everyone else into proper perspective. This looking to him is more than a passing glance. It really means coming to depend on him, transferring our trust to him, becoming joined to him. He's the one who gets us started in this life of faith. He is the source of the righteousness that becomes ours by faith. He is also the perfecter of our faith, meaning that he is at work in us developing the kind of faith that will enable us to face down disaster and still have joy. We look to Jesus because in him we see true reality, vastly unlike what we see on supposed reality television. We see the reality of his goodness in contrast to the world's wickedness. We see in his cross that in wrath, God has remembered mercy. We find in him the hope we need to endure whatever may come, trusting that he is strong enough and determined enough to get us safely home.

Looking Forward
If It Seems Slow, Wait for It

God gave his prophet Habakkuk a promise that the Babylonian captivity would be temporary and that after a set period of time God would deliver his people. But God anticipated that the years in between this promise and its fulfillment would seem very long. He told Habakkuk in advance that they were going to have to be willing to wait but that their waiting would not be in vain:

> For still the vision awaits its appointed time;
>   it hastens to the end—it will not lie.
> If it seems slow, wait for it;
>   it will surely come; it will not delay. (Hab. 2:3)

Habakkuk and the people of Judah were called to live by faith in the midst of great suffering, in the gap between promise and fulfillment. Similarly, the people of God in the first century were called to live by faith in the midst of great suffering, in the gap between promise and fulfillment. As the early church began to face acute persecution under a wicked ruler in Rome, they must have wondered, like Habakkuk, why God would allow it. A letter of encouragement made its way around to all of the struggling churches at the time. And interestingly, its message to them was the same message Habakkuk had written down long before, an encouragement to face with faith a future filled with difficulty. It says:

Recall the former days when, after you were enlightened, you endured a hard struggle with sufferings, sometimes being publicly exposed to reproach and affliction, and sometimes being partners with those so treated. For you had compassion on those in prison, and you joyfully accepted the plundering of your property, since you knew that you yourselves had a better possession and an abiding one. Therefore do not throw away your confidence, which has a great reward. For you have need of endurance, so that when you have done the will of God you may receive what is promised. For,

> Yet a little while,
>   and the coming one will come and will not delay;
> but my righteous one shall live by faith,
>   and if he shrinks back,
> my soul has no pleasure in him.

But we are not of those who shrink back and are destroyed, but of those who have faith and preserve their souls. (Heb. 10:32–39)

We, too, are living in the gap between promise and fulfillment. Like Habakkuk, we see injustice and violence all around us, and we wonder how long God will let it continue, how long he will put up with such wickedness in his world. We know Jesus left us with the promise that he will come again. We read Revelation 17 and 18 about the final judgment that will come upon Babylon, which represents the wicked ways of a world that hates God. We read about what it will be like in the New Jerusalem when God will bring his people into it. But we are here—in the midst of evil and suffering—still waiting for the promise to be fulfilled. Sometimes it seems slow. Yet we must wait for him. He will surely come. He will not delay.

Discussion Guide

Habakkuk

Getting the Discussion Going

1. Though we hate to admit it, we all have certain people we look at and say to ourselves, "I may not be perfect, but I'm better than them." Can you think of people or situations in which you struggle to understand how God could seemingly give a particular person or group the upper hand over "good people"?

Getting to the Heart of It

2. Did you notice what Habakkuk did with his frustration over God's seeming lack of concern and then what he did with his disappointment over God's seemingly unjust plan? How does this instruct us in regard to what we should do with our frustration and questions for God?

3. When Habakkuk heard that God was going to appoint the Babylonians to execute his judgment on Judah, he couldn't reconcile how a holy God could allow the wicked to swallow "the man more righteous than he" (Hab. 1:13). What we must come to understand in order to make sense of this?

4. Habakkuk was given a revelation that "awaits its appointed time" (Hab. 2:3). What was revealed to Habakkuk that he and the people of Judah would have to wait to see come to pass?

5. Habakkuk was given insight on what had happened in the past, which gave him confidence about the future (Hab. 3:1–5). What did God do in the past that Habakkuk anticipated God would do again?

6. Habakkuk asked God to remember mercy in his wrath. How did God answer that prayer for his people later exiled in Babylon? How did he answer that prayer when Christ died on the cross? How is he still answering that prayer today?

Getting Personal

7. In the Personal Bible Study you were asked to write your own version of what the prophet expressed in Habakkuk 3:17–19. Would some of you be willing to read your personal declaration of your intention to live by faith?

Getting How It Fits into the Big Picture

8. God gave Habakkuk the ability to see the day when "the earth will be filled with the knowledge of the glory of the LORD as the waters cover the sea" (Hab. 2:14). How is the earth being filled with the knowledge of the glory of the Lord today in a way it wasn't in his day? And how will the earth be filled with the knowledge of the Lord in an even greater way in the future?

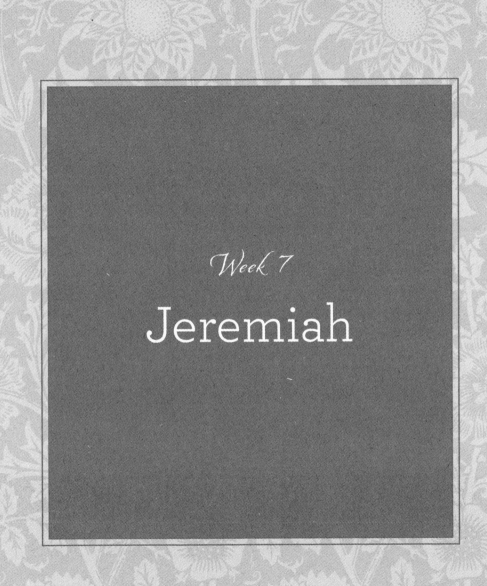

Week 7

Jeremiah

Jeremiah

1. Read Jeremiah 1:1–8 and list several things you learn about Jeremiah and his call to prophesy.

2. Jeremiah 1:10 summarizes Jeremiah's message throughout his forty years of prophetical ministry, using six key words that are repeated throughout Jeremiah's book (see also Jer. 18:7–11; 31:28; 45:4). What are these words, and what do you think they mean?

The Assyrian and Babylonian Empires (after Israel and Judah exile)

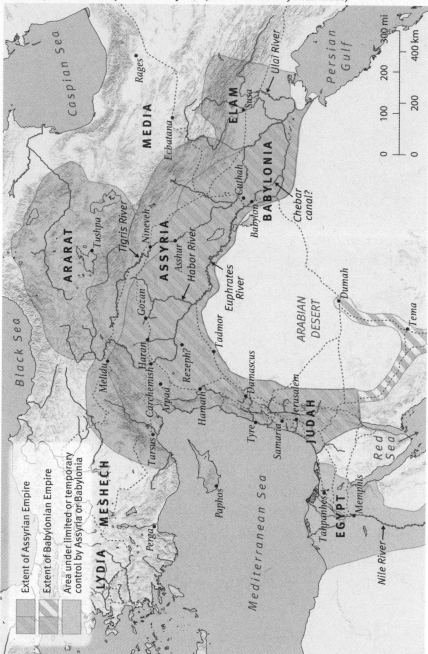

3. In addition to the six words about planting and building, God gave Jeremiah three pictures of what he could expect in regard to his prophetic ministry. What do you think is being communicated by each image in verses 1:11–19?

An almond branch (it is helpful to know that buds on almond trees were the first sign of spring in Judah):

A boiling pot facing away from the north:

A fortified city, an iron pillar, and bronze walls:

4. A few years into Jeremiah's prophetic ministry, something significant happened. Skim 2 Kings 22–23:25. Describe what happened in two or three sentences.

5. Jeremiah 2 is representative of the message of Jeremiah during Josiah's reign. The chapter begins with God's fondly remembering the love his people once had for him as his bride in the wilderness. But then he begins to work his way through all the good reasons he now

has cause to divorce his bride. Summarize his charges against Judah, found in the following verses:

2:4–8

2:10–12

2:18–19

2:20–22

2:23–25

2:26–28

2:34–35

6. Sadly, the reforms Josiah brought in Judah lasted only as long as Josiah was king. When his son took his place on the throne, Judah went back to all of her evils of the past. What was the source of the problem, according to Jeremiah 3:10?

7. Jeremiah becomes more specific about the problem in Jeremiah 17. What is the problem, according to Jeremiah 17:1, 9–10?

8. In Jeremiah 25 we have "the word that came to Jeremiah concerning all the people of Judah, in the fourth year of Jehoiakim the son of Josiah, king of Judah" (v. 1). Read Jeremiah 25:1–14 and summarize in a sentence or two what Jeremiah says is going to happen and why.

9. In Jeremiah 30–33, after many chapters about the sins of Judah and the judgment to come upon her, Jeremiah speaks of what is to come beyond the exile, when God will act to restore his people. How is God promising to bring restoration in each of the following verses?

30:3

30: 8–9

30:17

30:19

30:22

31:4

31:5

31:8–9

31:12–14

31:27–28

31:31

31:38–40

10. In Jeremiah 31:33–34, Jeremiah details four aspects of the new covenant. What are they?

11. Jeremiah says that the new covenant will not be like the covenant God had made with Israel at Mount Sinai, when he gave them his law. This leads us to ask how it will be different. Work your way through the following verses to discover what makes the new covenant superior to the old covenant.

	Old Covenant	New Covenant
Mediator	Ex. 20:18–19; Heb. 9:19–20	Heb. 8:6; 9:15
Ratification	Ex. 24:8; Heb. 9:18–20	Matt. 26:28
Obligations	Deut. 13:4	Rom. 3:21–25
Promises	Ex. 19:5; Deut. 28:1–14	Jer. 31:33–34; Heb. 12:12, 15
Conditions	Ex. 19:5–6; Deut. 30:16–17	John 5:24; Rom. 10:6–11
Where written	Deut. 4:13	Jer. 31:33
Relationship with God	Heb. 5:1	Jer. 31:34; Heb. 4:14–16
Way of dealing with sin	Heb. 9:9–10; 10:2–4	Jer. 31:34; Heb. 9:14, 26; 10:10, 14, 18

Teaching Chapter

I Pledge My Allegiance

One of the solid fixtures of my summers growing up was vacation Bible school. There was the making of salt maps and papier-mâché projects and building things with popsicle sticks and much playing and singing and Oreo-eating. Every day of vacation Bible school began with saying the pledge of allegiance—really three pledges of allegiance, one to the American flag, another to the Christian flag, and then a pledge to the Bible. We said, "I pledge allegiance to the Bible, God's Holy Word. I will make it a light unto my feet and a lamp unto my path. I will hide its words in my heart that I may not sin against God." Evidently it was all about me—my study to know what it said, my diligence in memorizing it, my determination to obey it. "I will do this," was my pledge.

God's Law Written on Stone

Really, it was the same pledge the people of God made the first time they heard God's law. When God descended upon Mount Sinai and inscribed his law onto stone tablets, Moses took them down to the people and read it to them. There they pledged their allegiance. They said, "All that the LORD has spoken we will do, and we will be obedient" (Ex. 24:7). Forty years later Moses stood before the next generation of Israelites, who were preparing to cross over the Jordan to make their home in Canaan. There, Moses pulled out those stone tablets—inscribed by the finger of God himself—and began working his way through them: "You shall have no other gods before me. You shall not make for yourself a carved image. . . . You shall not take the name of the LORD your God in vain. . . . Observe the Sabbath day. . . . Honor your father and your mother. . . . You shall not murder. . . . You shall not commit adultery. . . . You shall not steal. . . . You shall not bear false witness. . . . You shall not covet" (Deut. 5:7–21). Moses continued:

> These words that I command you today shall be on your heart. You shall teach them diligently to your children. (Deut. 6:6–7)

From the very beginning, God's people were to know God's law. But it wasn't supposed to be just something outside of them, imposed on them. It was supposed to be on their heart—at the center of who they were, the very heartbeat of their lives, something they cherished as it brought and bound them to the God who had saved them from Egypt to love and worship him.

Moses wrote down clear instructions for the day when God would give Israel a king:

> And when he sits on the throne of his kingdom, he shall write for himself in a book a copy of this law, approved by the Levitical priests. And it shall be with him, and he shall read in it all the days of his life, that he may learn to fear the LORD his God by keeping all the words of this law and these statutes, and doing them, that his heart may not be lifted up above his brothers, and that he may not turn aside from the commandment, either to the right hand or to the left, so that he may continue long in his kingdom, he and his children, in Israel. (Deut. 17:18–20)

The king over God's people wasn't just supposed to read the book that Moses wrote—the Book of the Law, or, as we call it, Deuteronomy. The king was supposed to write out a copy for himself and get it checked off by the priest. Every day of his life and every decree of his government were to be shaped by God's law. This would keep him humble and holy and would make him a blessing to God's people.

Fast-forward eight hundred years, when there was a new king on the throne over the southern kingdom of Judah named Josiah. His grandfather, Manasseh, had been the most evil king ever to rule over Judah. Manasseh had built altars to Baal and Asherah, not just somewhere around Jerusalem but right in God's house, the temple. Instead of teaching God's commands diligently to his children, he had burned one of his sons as an offering to a false god. He had brought fortune-tellers and people who consulted the dead into the palace. Needless to say, he did not begin and end each day reading from a copy of Book of the Law. In fact, during the time Manasseh was king, the Book of the Law was completely lost. No one in Israel was reading it. No one was teaching it to their children.

Now, I have to stop to admit here that I have often misplaced my Bible. There have been more Sunday mornings than I would care to admit when I've gone to look for my Bible to take to church with me and realized it was still in the car with the bulletin stuck in it from the previous Sunday. A whole week had gone by, and I hadn't read it. Worse than that, I hadn't even missed it. So now you know how I've done with my pledge of allegiance to the Bible.

The Book of the Law had been lost for many years when Manasseh's grandson, Josiah, at only eight years old, came to the throne. About the time eight-year-old Josiah began to reign in Jerusalem, a baby was born to the high priest, a baby named Jeremiah. And just as Josiah became a king when he was only eight years old, so Jeremiah became a prophet when he was only thirteen years old. He writes about that day:

> Now the word of the LORD came to me, saying,
>
> > "Before I formed you in the womb I knew you,
> > and before you were born I consecrated you;
> > I appointed you a prophet to the nations."
>
> Then I said, "Ah, Lord GOD! Behold, I do not know how to speak, for I am only a youth." But the LORD said to me,
>
> > "Do not say, 'I am only a youth';
> > for to all to whom I send you, you shall go,
> > and whatever I command you, you shall speak." (Jer. 1:4–7)

A few years later, Josiah the king had carpenters and masons working at the temple to restore it, and he sent over his secretary to deliver some money for timber and stone. When the secretary arrived at the temple, Hilkiah the high priest had some incredible news:

> Hilkiah the high priest said to Shaphan the secretary, "I have found the Book of the Law in the house of the LORD." (2 Kings 22:8)

When Hilkiah found the Book of the Law, it had been missing not for a week or a month or even a year but for at least sixty years. It is hard to imagine how something so important, so precious, was lost in what was really a rather small space. But evidently they hadn't missed it. Josiah had been king at this point for eighteen years, but he had never heard or read the Scriptures. When he finally did hear it, he tore his clothes in grief and despair. It was like a mirror had been held up in front of the king in which he could see the rebellion in the hearts of God's people, the idolatry that pervaded the land, as well as the compromise in his own life. So he called all the people together.

> And he read in their hearing all the words of the Book of the Covenant that had been found in the house of the LORD. And the king stood by the pillar and made a covenant before the LORD, to walk after the LORD and to keep his commandments and his testimonies and his statutes with all his heart and all his soul, to perform the words of this covenant that were written in this book. And all the people joined in the covenant. (2 Kings 23:2–3)

So King Josiah, with the prophet Jeremiah at his side, began a crusade of reformation throughout Judah. All of the vessels for Baal and Asherah worship came out of the temple. All the priests appointed for idol worship were deposed. The houses of male cult prostitutes were torn down. The places where children were burned in the fire as an offering to Molech were covered over. The altars built for the foreign gods were destroyed. Josiah reinstituted the celebration of the Passover, which hadn't been kept since the days of the judges.

These were great days in Judah. There was a fresh knowledge of God's law and a commitment to keep it as well as a renewed observance of religious feasts. But there was a problem. We discover what it was in Jeremiah 3:10: "Yet . . . Judah did not return to me with her

whole heart, but in pretense, declares the LORD." All the outward con-
formity to a new sheriff in town was just that. There was no real inner
change. Josiah's reforms lasted only as long as Josiah. Josiah died, and
his son Jehoiakim became king. And whereas Josiah had mourned over
Judah's sin and sought to bring his people under obedience to God's
law, Jehoiakim had a very different response when the Scriptures were
read to him:

> It was the ninth month, and the king was sitting in the winter house, and
> there was a fire burning in the fire pot before him. As Jehudi read three or
> four columns, the king would cut them off with a knife and throw them
> into the fire in the fire pot, until the entire scroll was consumed in the
> fire that was in the fire pot. Yet neither the king nor any of his servants
> who heard all these words was afraid, nor did they tear their garments.
> (Jer. 36:22–24)

In the coldness of this room, there was no warmth for God's Word. No
sadness over sin. No reverent fear. No ears to hear. No heart to obey. We
can almost hear them laughing at what they were reading as they cut
up God's Word page by page and threw it in the fire.

In the days of the kings over Israel and Judah, as went the king, so
went the people. And within a few short years, all the altars to foreign
gods that Josiah had torn down had been rebuilt. All the practices of
worshiping Baal had been reinstated. "Jeremiah must have wondered
at that point, *If all that Josiah did couldn't change the hearts of the people,
what will?*"[12]

And isn't this really the story of the entirety of the Old Testament?
The people had God's law; they had God dwelling with them in the tabernacle and later in the temple. They had the land that God had given to
them. They had the sacrifices and the feasts and the priesthood. They
made grand promises to obey, but they could never seem to keep them.
They could never keep their hearts true to God alone. What was the
problem with these people? Jeremiah diagnosed it in chapter 17. And
it is not just the diagnosis of the problem in the people of Jeremiah's
day. It's our problem, too. Jeremiah's diagnosis reveals the fundamental problem of the human heart in every age.

Sin Engraved on the Heart

> The heart is deceitful above all things,
> and desperately sick;
> who can understand it? (Jer. 17:9)

Jeremiah is seemingly given X-ray vision into the hearts—the inner disposition—of his people, where he can see the problem clearly:

> The sin of Judah is written with a pen of iron; with a point of diamond it is engraved on the tablet of their heart. (Jer. 17:1)

It is as if someone has taken the tool of a tattoo artist and inked onto Judah's heart the names of all her sins: idolatry, adultery, murder. It's as if a photographer had been following the people of Judah around, taking pictures at the houses of the male cult prostitutes and at Topheth, where they'd thrown children into the fire, and then posted the photographs all over the walls of her heart like concert posters plastered on bulletin boards and telephone poles around a college campus. The walls of her heart were covered with the photographic evidence. She couldn't get away from it. It was all there, defining not only her past failures but also her present reality. It wasn't the commandments of God, which Moses so long ago said should be upon her heart, that had come to define the culture of her heart, but instead a vivid record of her sin.

And isn't it the same with us? Don't we have hearts engraved with a record of all the ways we have broken every command? It's all there, written with a pen of iron, deeply engrained in who we are, our breaking of every command. We've bowed down before the god of our reputation. We've worshiped the carved images of rail-thin, perfect-skinned, stylishly dressed celebrities. We've put on spiritual talk when it suited our purposes, taking the Lord's name in vain. We've spent Sundays at the soccer field and football stadium and hockey rink rather than reserving them for enjoying the Lord. We've been unfaithful to our spouse, if only in our imagination. We've rolled our eyes at the wisdom of our parents, and exaggerated the faults of others, and burned with jealousy over what someone else has that we don't.

What sin has been engraved on the tablet of your heart? What pictures are posted there of your disobedience to God's commands? Is there is a picture engraved on your heart of your ridiculing rather than respecting your parents, a picture of the abortion clinic you went to, or the personal business you've done on company time, or the person whose reputation you ruined with your words? Is there a printout of your critical, cynical thoughts? Is there a photo of the position, the family, the house, the body, or the success someone else has that you covet? More importantly, is there anything or anyone that can take these words and images away? Or are we destined to be defined by the sin engraved on our hearts forever?

Jeremiah said that Judah's sin was not only engraved on her heart; it was also "on the horns of their altars" (Jer. 17:1). The altar was the place of God's presence. Our sin is not just plastered all over our hearts; it has come before the face of God.

This is something King David understood. David tried for some time to ignore the sin that had been engraved on his heart, the pictures of it posted there of his adultery with Bathsheba and the murder of Uriah. But then, confronted by Nathan, David saw his sin for what it was. "My sin is ever before me," he said (Ps. 51:3). He recognized that even though he had sinned against many people, his sin was primarily against God, so he said, "Against you, you only, have I sinned" (v. 4). He not only wanted to be forgiven; he wanted to be cleansed. So he begged, "Create in me a clean heart, O God, and renew a right spirit within me" (v. 10). He knew that if God didn't do something in his heart, if God did not clean away all the words and images that had come to define the culture of his heart, he would just keep on sinning in the same ways. David also knew that his sin was before a holy and just God and that it had to be paid for. It was there on the horns of the altar. A sacrifice was going to have to be offered; blood was going to have to be shed. Yet David seemed to grasp that a more perfect and pervasive remedy for sin was needed, writing, "For you will not delight in sacrifice, or I would give it; you will not be pleased with a burnt offering" (v. 16). David longed for the day when the once-for-all more perfect sacrifice would be offered that would cleanse away his sin.

God had made clear that the only way the people could be the way he wanted them to be was if they were to work his law into the fabric of their hearts. But that just hadn't happened. Fear of judgment didn't change their hearts. Religious ritual didn't change their hearts. The law had proved powerless to bring about any kind of lasting change.

Jeremiah saw the unrepentant sin on the hearts and in the lives of his people. And, worse, he saw what was about to happen because of that sin, as Babylon made inroads into Judah, taking her people away into exile. He laments:

> For the wound of the daughter of my people is my heart wounded;
>   I mourn, and dismay has taken hold on me.
>
> Is there no balm in Gilead?
>   Is there no physician there?
> Why then has the health of the daughter of my people
>   not been restored? (Jer. 8:21–22)

Jeremiah's heart was broken over the condition of the hearts of God's people. He wondered why God, the healer, had not done something to remedy the sin sickness of their hearts. Perhaps you can relate. You had thought that by now you would have figured out how to say no to that same old sin. Perhaps you've come to realize that the only way you are ever going to change is if God does some kind of miracle. God is going to have to do something. Something big. Jeremiah ached with longing for God to do something—something big—that would bring the healing and restoration his people desperately needed. And finally, the day came when God revealed to Jeremiah exactly what he was going to do.

> I will restore the fortunes of my people, Israel and Judah, says the LORD, and I will bring them back to the land that I gave to their fathers, and they shall take possession of it. (Jer. 30:3)

God revealed to Jeremiah that he was going to bring his people back to the land where he had always intended to dwell with them. He went on to say that he was going to rescue them from the yoke of slavery in Babylon so they could serve him (Jer. 30:8–9). He's going to heal their incurable wound (v. 17), rebuild their city from the rubble (v. 18), multiply them (v. 19), punish those who have oppressed them (v. 20), and give them a king who will love the Lord (v. 21). He's going to claim them as his own and give himself to them (v. 22).

And that's not all. With this promise of restoration of the land and the nation came the promise of a much deeper, a much more personal and individual, restoration as well. This was what generations who preceded Jeremiah and generations that would come after him longed to hear. This was the answer to their inability to live up to their pledge of allegiance to impress his Word on their hearts so they would not sin against him.

God's Law Written on the Heart

> Behold, the days are coming, declares the LORD, when I will make a new covenant with the house of Israel and the house of Judah, not like the covenant that I made with their fathers on the day when I took them by the hand to bring them out of the land of Egypt, my covenant that they broke, though I was their husband, declares the LORD. (Jer. 31:31–32)

God made a covenant with his people at Mount Sinai when he gave them the Ten Commandments and the rest of the law, which is called the "old covenant." The people of Israel there that day pledged to obey it. Throughout the years future generations recommitted to obeying it, as they did in Josiah's day. But they didn't obey it. They never seemed to follow through on their determination to obey. But now, in this prophecy from Jeremiah, God promises that the day will come when he will make a new covenant with them that will be different from the one he made at Mount Sinai with their forefathers. How will it be different?

> For this is the covenant that I will make with the house of Israel after those days, declares the LORD: I will put my law within them, and I will write it on their hearts. And I will be their God, and they shall be my people. And no longer shall each one teach his neighbor and each his brother, saying, "Know the LORD," for they shall all know me, from the least of them to the greatest, declares the LORD. For I will forgive their iniquity, and I will remember their sin no more. (Jer. 31:33–34)

The way sin will be dealt with will be different. The way people will relate to God will be different. The people's power to obey the law will be different. Let's look at each of these.

Sin will be dealt with in a different way in the new covenant. For centuries the people had made their treks to the temple with their ram or goat or bird to offer a sacrifice for sin, yet it didn't deal with sin in any final way. They would sin again and have to make another trip to the temple. But in the new covenant to come, their sin, which was there on the horns of the altar, would be atoned for through a single once-for-all sacrifice. All the sins of their past, their present, and their future would be fully and finally dealt with so that no further sacrifice would be required. Their sin won't just be covered over; it will be removed, never to be remembered again by the one they have sinned against.

People will relate to God in a different way. Under the old covenant, human priests served as mediators between the people and God. The priests entered into the presence of God in the temple on their behalf, but ordinary people could never come near. The prophets heard messages from God and communicated God's word to them, but ordinary Israelites didn't have a sense of God's speaking to them directly or personally. But under the new covenant, there will be no unique tribe or class of people serving as mediators. Rather, there will be one mediator between God and man. Jesus himself will intercede for them before the throne of God. Jesus himself will speak to them directly through his Word as his Spirit illumines and applies it to them. He will invite them to draw near to God based on his perfect record of holiness.

There will also be a new ability to obey God's law, provided for in the new covenant. Moses had lamented centuries earlier, as God's people prepared to cross over into the Promised Land, that "to this day the Lord has not given you a heart to understand or eyes to see or ears to hear" (Deut. 29:4). Moses longed for God to do what Jeremiah heard God promising he would do. God was going to give his people a new power to understand and obey him that would be far greater than God's people had ever experienced under the old covenant. He was going to do the miracle they had always longed for. He was going to do something big. He's not only going to remove the sin that had been engraved on their hearts; he's going to write his law on their hearts.

Perhaps that doesn't sound like good news to you. Perhaps it sounds unduly authoritarian to think that God intends to write his law on your tender heart. Perhaps it sounds like the tattoo of a prison camp. But if that's what you think, then you've never truly understood the gracious foundation and nature of God's law. God's law is first and foremost a revelation of his character. The law is what it is because he is who he is. His writing his law on our hearts means that his desires will become our desires instead of remaining an external set of rules. He will implant within us a new set and range of desires so that what we will want most is for our lives to conform to his beauty and joy and goodness. God promises that he will turn the prevailing disposition of our souls away from all the things that have brought us only disappointment and misery and toward everything that will make us holy and happy forever.

Jeremiah wrote down this almost too-good-to-be-true promise in his book. The people read about this promise throughout the centuries. And finally the day came when this promise became the actual experience of God's people:

> When the day of Pentecost arrived, they were all together in one place. And suddenly there came from heaven a sound like a mighty rushing wind, and it filled the entire house where they were sitting. And divided tongues as of fire appeared to them and rested on each one of them. And they were all filled with the Holy Spirit and began to speak in other tongues as the Spirit gave them utterance. (Acts 2:1–4)

Interestingly, the new covenant was delivered and ratified in some surprisingly similar and also dissimilar ways to the old covenant. When God gave the old covenant in the days of Moses, he descended in fire and wrapped Sinai in smoke (Ex. 19:18). On the day of Pentecost, God descended in fire, but this time his fiery presence rested on believers, a visible manifestation of his coming to dwell not in a tabernacle or temple made of stone, but in the hearts and lives of his people by his Spirit. At Mount Sinai, Moses ascended the mountain, then descended with the Ten Commandments, inscribed in stone, in his hands. Just prior to Pentecost, Christ ascended into the presence of God, and on the Day of Pentecost he descended by his Spirit, not to deliver tablets of stone but to write God's law on the hearts of believers.

Pentecost was "the day" Jeremiah wrote about, the day he said was coming when the promise of the new covenant would be fulfilled. From that day on, the Holy Spirit not only reminded his people of God's Word but also gave them the ability to understand it and the power to obey it. The Spirit came down to work through the Word so that you and I can be transformed by the renewal of our minds, able to discern what is the will of God, what is good and acceptable and perfect (Rom. 12:2).

Back at Sinai, when God gave the old covenant through Moses, Moses took the blood of an ox and threw it on the people and said, "Behold the blood of the covenant that the LORD has made with you in accordance with all these words" (Ex. 24:8). The new covenant, however, was ratified by the blood of a far superior sacrifice.

> He took bread, and when he had given thanks, he broke it and gave it to them, saying, "This is my body, which is given for you. Do this in remembrance of me." And likewise the cup after they had eaten, saying, "This cup that is poured out for you is the new covenant in my blood." (Luke 22:19–20)

When Jesus said, "the new covenant," all of the disciples in the upper room, who had heard the prophecy of Jeremiah read throughout their lives, would have made the connection. Finally, God's promise through Jeremiah of the new covenant was becoming a reality. The writer of Hebrews makes it explicit, saying of Jesus:

> Therefore he is the mediator of a new covenant. . . . He has appeared once for all at the end of the ages to put away sin by the sacrifice of himself. (Heb. 9:15, 26)

Jesus came into the world; he has come to you to put away your sin so that it doesn't have to rule you and condemn you anymore. Can you see him now, by his Holy Spirit who has taken up residence within you, putting away your sin, pulling down the pictures, rubbing out the words written there that have defined you? This is the restoration that Jeremiah had promised. All the thoughts and desires and habits that shaped your inner life and led only to misery are even now being replaced with new thoughts about what is worthwhile, new desires to please him, a new hunger for his Word, and new habits of preferring God.

Those Ten Commandments are becoming more than a poster on the wall of our Sunday school classroom. He's writing his law on our hearts. He is, even now, giving us eyes to see his beauty and the ugliness of everything else we have bowed down to so that we want to worship him alone. He is developing in us a sensitivity against using his name for selfish purposes. He is instilling in us a radical trust in his provision so that we can enjoy Sabbath rest instead of making the Lord's Day a catch-up day. He is taking away the old resentments and giving us a new tenderness toward our parents and a willingness to give weight to their words. He is giving us a new reverence for life, a fresh commitment to faithfulness, a new awareness of our subtle ways of stealing, a new integrity in our words about other people, a new sense of contentment with what we've been given. He is writing his law on our hearts. It's a miracle.

You can try as hard as you want to change, but you can't accomplish this kind of change on your own. This is a work God does through his Word by his Spirit. When God works this miracle in your heart, you find that you want to know him in a way you just weren't interested in before. You find the Bible to be curiously inviting rather than boring. You feel drawn to Christ instead of wanting to keep him at a safe distance. You find yourself grateful for conviction rather than resistant to it.

What's wrong with the human heart? It has been pasted over with patterns of resistance and rebellion. What needs to happen? Certainly something more than putting our hands over our hearts and pledging our allegiance. The gracious law of God must be written there by his Spirit, replacing all the sin that has been engraved on it. How will that happen? It happens only when the life of God is implanted through a secret miracle in the human soul, a miracle called "regeneration." The miracle continues through the ongoing process of sanctification. We open ourselves up to this miracle when we say, *Lord, I find I am powerless to change the fundamental disposition of my own soul. I simply don't have it in me to keep all these external rules. They are no match for the mainspring of motivation in my heart, which is to please me and not you. I am in need of nothing less than a miracle here. I need for you to heal the wound sin has left on my soul. I need for you to create a new heart within me so that I won't keep walking in the same deep grooves engraved on my heart by years of habitual sin. I need the permanent presence of your Spirit to provide me with power to do ongoing battle with all of the old sin habits that keep crying out to me. I need for you to implant within me the new spiritual life that only you can give.*

The good news of the gospel is not that you must pledge your allegiance to the Bible (though the Bible is worthy of your allegiance and diligence and intelligence). The good news of the gospel is that God has pledged his allegiance to all who turn toward him in faith and repentance. His Spirit will illumine your reading of his Word so that it will be a light to your feet and a lamp to your path. He will write his loving law on your heart so that what you will want more than anything is to no longer sin against him.

Looking Forward
I Will Restore

Jeremiah promised a people who were experiencing the loss of everything they held dear that the day would come when God would restore it all, and that the restoration would, in fact, be even better than what they had lost. In addition to restoring them to the land they called "home" and the life they enjoyed there, God promised to restore their freedom, their health, their purity, and their honor (Jeremiah 30). God promised a new covenant in which they would experience a new ability to obey and relate to God and a new freedom of forgiveness (Jer. 31:31–34). He promised that the city of Jerusalem that they loved would be rebuilt. "It shall not be plucked up or overthrown anymore forever" (Jer. 31:38–40).

The fulfillment of these promises of restoration began when the exiles from Babylon made their way back to Jerusalem. Under Nehemiah's leadership, God's people built a new city on the ruins of the old. But certainly the restoration they experienced came nowhere close to the magnificent promises God had made through his prophet Jeremiah.

Then Christ came and inaugurated the new covenant, making forgiveness possible by shedding his blood and pouring out his Spirit upon his people to create in them a new immediacy in relating to God and a new power for obeying him. Yet this was still not all that God promised through Jeremiah. Although God is writing his law on our hearts, we still struggle with sin. We still long for the day when sin will be gone for good, when we will sin no more.

While we now have the ability to know God and belong to him in a way that is far superior to the saints in Jeremiah's day, we long for the day when we will relate to him face-to-face. He is doing his rebuilding work, as we, as living stones, are being built into a temple where he will dwell. On that day we will hear a loud voice from the throne telling us that what was promised through Jeremiah has come to full fruition. The loud voice will say, "Behold, the dwelling place of God is with man. He will dwell with them, and they will be his people, and God himself will be with them as their God" (Rev. 21:3).

On the day when Christ returns, the Spirit's work of writing his law on our hearts will be complete. He who began a good work in us will have been faithful to complete it (Phil. 1:6). All the people of God will be gathered together, healed and whole, purified and glorified, in the New Jerusalem. And we will never have to fear being exiled from God's presence or alienated from him because of sin. We will be planted, sacred to the Lord, never to be uprooted or overthrown anymore forever.

Discussion Guide

Jeremiah

Getting the Discussion Going

1. What do you think about Jeremiah's observation of the human heart, that it is deceitful above all things and desperately sick? How does this fit with the prevailing wisdom that says people are basically good?

Getting to the Heart of It

2. In the Personal Bible Study we saw that Jeremiah's prophetic ministry was centered on God's promises to pluck up, break down, destroy, overthrow, build, and plant. How did that happen in Judah's actual experience as a nation?

3. What do you think about the image of sin as being engraved on the human heart? How does this imagery help us to grasp the impulse to sin, the tyranny of sin, and the difficulty we have in turning away from sin?

4. How would you explain the difference between having God's law written on tablets of stone, which you have to impress on your own heart, and having it written on your heart by the Holy Spirit?

5. Imagine that you were a Jew living in Jerusalem at Pentecost. You heard Peter's sermon and were one of those who was "cut to the heart,

and said to Peter and the rest of the apostles, 'Brothers, what shall we do?'" (Acts 2:37). How would your life change as you began to live as a partaker of the new covenant instead of the old covenant?

6. While God has begun his work in our hearts, giving us new hearts to obey him, the reality is that we still struggle with sin. Clearly there are still some deep impressions left on our lives by sin that will not be completely gone until "he who began a good work" in us "will bring it to completion at the day of Jesus Christ" (Phil. 1:6). If we are experiencing an ongoing struggle with sin, is that evidence that perhaps we have not experienced this miracle of the new birth? Why or why not?

Getting Personal

7. Let's open our Bibles to the Ten Commandments found in Deuteronomy 5. When you look over this list of commands, can you give testimony to the way in which the Holy Spirit has worked in your life to write one of these on your heart? How have you experienced God at work, giving you the desire and the power to obey one of these commands?

Getting How It Fits into the Big Picture

8. The story of the Bible begins in the garden of Eden where everything was good. Then Adam and Eve sinned, and the world became filled with dysfunction, disorder, disease, disobedience, and death. But right there in the garden God promised that the seed of the woman would one day crush the head of the seed of the Serpent so that the perfection of the garden paradise would be restored. Look back at the promises of restoration God made in Jeremiah 30–31 that you listed in the Personal Bible Study. How did these predictions of the glorious state of blessing after the exile begin to be fulfilled at Christ's first coming, how have they continued to be fulfilled in part today, and how will they finally be realized beyond imagination when Christ returns?

Week 8

Daniel

Daniel

Up to this point, all the prophets we've studied have been prophesying to the northern kingdom of Israel or the southern kingdom of Judah prior to Israel's exile to Assyria and Judah's exile to Babylon. The message of the prophets has usually included a call to the people to repent so that the people would not face exile. But when we come to Daniel, the time for that has passed. The setting of Daniel is Babylon, where the people of Judah are living in exile.

Daniel can be divided into two halves. The first six chapters of Daniel tell us the story of Daniel and his three friends, Shadrach, Meshach, and Abednego, who as teenagers were in the first of three waves of exiles taken from Jerusalem to Babylon. The second half of the book, chapters 7 through 12, presents to us the visions Daniel had regarding the future. Though the two halves are very different kinds of literature, each section helps us to understand the other. The two distinct halves of the book of Daniel combine to show God's people how to live as strangers and exiles in a world that is not their home and to reassure them that God is in control and that his kingdom will ultimately prevail over the kingdoms of the world.

1. Read Daniel 1:1–2. If you were a citizen of Jerusalem trusting in Yahweh, what would you find troubling about what is revealed in these first two verses of Daniel?

2. Read Daniel 1:3–7. From these verses list four or five things the king of Babylon did and what his strategy or goal for each of them might have been.

3. Read Daniel 1:8–21. Why do you think Daniel asked that he and his friends be able to eat vegetables instead of the king's food? (Notice this is a "why do you think" question, since there may be a number of possible reasons.) What kind of impact do you think that had on them and those around them?

4. Read the account of Nebuchadnezzar's dream and Daniel's interpretation of it in Daniel 2. How would you summarize the point of the dream, according to Daniel 2:36–45?

5. What light does the parable Jesus told in Luke 20:9–18 and the words of Peter in Acts 4:10–12 shed on who or what the "stone . . . cut out by no human hand" might be?

6. Certainly Shadrach, Meshach, and Abednego knew about Nebuchadnezzar's dream of the great image that represented successive human kingdoms being crushed by the "stone . . . cut out by no human hand" (Dan. 2:34). How do you think that image might have played a part in their refusal to bow down to the image Nebuchadnezzar set up, as recorded in chapter 3?

7. According to Nebuchadnezzar, Shadrach, Meshach, and Abednego were accompanied in the fire by one "like a son of the gods" (Dan. 3:25) and emerged with the hair of their heads unsinged, cloaks unharmed, and no smell of smoke. What does this reveal about the nature of God's deliverance?

8. In Daniel 5 we read about a new king in Babylon, Belshazzar, holding a great feast, when a human hand appeared and wrote on the wall of the palace. According to verses 24–30, what was the message, and what was the result?

9. Daniel was likely in his eighties or nineties at the time of the events described in Daniel 6. What evidence do you see in this story that his determination not to defile himself and to retain his identity as a citizen of Jerusalem (revealed in Daniel 1) has continued throughout his life?

10. Daniel's experience of facing the lion's den prefigures Jesus's experience of facing the cross. Write a sentence about Jesus in the second column below that parallels the sentence about Daniel in the first column.

Daniel	Jesus
Though Daniel was living in the kingdom of Babylon, he was from the kingdom of Judah. (Dan. 1:3–4)	John 6:33; 18:36
Daniel was without fault yet opposed by envious leaders who corrupted the justice system to condemn him. (Dan. 6:5–10)	Mark 14:1, 55, 64
Darius wanted to release Daniel instead of sending him to the lions' den. (Dan. 6:14)	Luke 23:13–16
Daniel is not recorded as having said anything in his defense. (Dan. 6:16)	Mark 15:5

Daniel was placed in a den, or cave, which was sealed with a stone so that he could not be saved by human intervention. (Dan. 6:17)	Matt. 27:59–66
Daniel willingly faced the threat of death. (Dan. 6:10, 19)	Matt. 26:39
When the stone was removed, Daniel came out of the den, metaphorically brought back from the dead. (Dan. 6:23)	Matt. 28:5; 1 Cor. 15:3–4
When Daniel emerged from the lions' den, he came alone. No one else was saved by God's deliverance of Daniel. (Dan. 6:23)	1 Cor. 15:20–24
All of those who opposed Daniel perished in the lion's den. (Dan. 6:24)	John 15:6; Rev. 20:15

11. Daniel's vision of four great beasts in chapter 7 parallels the dream King Nebuchadnezzar had in chapter 2 in its revelation of the future course of history in regard to the kingdoms of the world and the kingdom of God. Read Daniel 7:1–18. Looking past the details of the vision, what would you say is its primary impression or message?

Teaching Chapter

What You Need to Know

Certain cities evoke a certain way of life, a certain set of values, don't they? Just the name of some cities makes us think of what is important to those who live there and what life is like. Think, for example, about Paris, Rome, Beijing, Toyko, Moscow, New York, Los Angeles.

In many ways we could say that the Bible presents to us the story of two great cities. These two cities have their own ethos, their own lifestyle, values, and convictions. They have very different origins, very different leaders, and dramatically different futures. The Bible, from beginning to end, is the story of Jerusalem, the city of God, and Babylon, the city of man. These two cities, and the tension between them, takes center stage in the book of Daniel.

We can trace the city of Babylon back to its roots in the story of the tower of Babel found in Genesis 11, where the people determined to build a great city and a great name for themselves. Babylon has always stood for human achievement and independence from God. Babylon is proud of its own power, satisfied in its own accomplishments, and secure in its self-made structures. Whenever and wherever human beings build a way of life with themselves at the center, it is really Babylon all over again.

Jerusalem, in stark contrast to Babylon, was the city God built, the city God chose for his people to dwell in, the city in which he enthroned his representative on earth, the king of Israel. God himself descended to dwell among the people he loves in the city of Jerusalem. This is the city through which God intends to accomplish his purposes to bless the whole world.

With this background, what we find in the first verses of Daniel's book is very troubling:

> In the third year of the reign of Jehoiakim king of Judah, Nebuchadnezzar king of Babylon came to Jerusalem and besieged it. And the Lord gave Jehoiakim king of Judah into his hand, with some of the vessels of the house of God. And he brought them to the land of Shinar, to the house of his god, and placed the vessels in the treasury of his god. (Dan. 1:1–2)

This turn of events is almost too much to take in if you understand what Babylon had always been and what Jerusalem was always meant to be. The king of Babylon had attacked the city of Jerusalem and won. The powers of the world appear to have defeated the glory of God. That's hard enough. But then we read that this was due not to mere military might but to something God did. Lest we think only the king and the people of Jerusalem were impacted, we are told right away that the very temple where God dwelt was violated. The king of Babylon had taken away some of the vessels (meaning the goblets stored on the table of the presence in the Holy Place of the temple that were used for drink offerings), and he had stashed them in the temple dedicated to his false god back in Babylon. And it's not just the goblets from the temple in Jerusalem that the king of Babylon had transported to Babylon:

> Then the king commanded Ashpenaz, his chief eunuch, to bring some of the people of Israel, both of the royal family and of the nobility, youths without blemish, of good appearance and skillful in all wisdom, endowed with knowledge, understanding learning, and competent to stand in the king's palace, and to teach them the literature and language of the Chaldeans. (Dan. 1:3–4)

The king of Babylon sent his men into the homes of Jerusalem to round up the best and brightest young men, young enough, he hoped, not to be so set in the ways of Jerusalem that they would resist the ways of Babylon when they got there. These royal sons of Jerusalem were taken five hundred miles east to live in Babylon. At the outset of this book, we wonder, as readers, what will happen to these young citizens of Jerusalem when they are taken to live in Babylon. That is really the big question the book of Daniel addresses: How does a person live in Babylon as a citizen of Jerusalem?

And this was not just a question of concern to those people in that time. It is the question that God's people, living as exiles in this world today, have to ask and answer. The book of Hebrews calls us "strangers and exiles on the earth," people for whom God has prepared a city, the New Jerusalem. (Heb. 11:13–16; see also Rev. 21:1). So how are we to live our lives in this world without withdrawing from the world and yet not becoming just like the world? How are we going to be a blessing to the world and yet resist being pressed into its mold? The stories and the visions of the book of Daniel work together to reveal to us what we must know if we want to live wisely in the kingdom of the world as citizens of the kingdom of God.

You've Got to Know Who You Really Are

In Daniel 1 we discover that to live wisely in the kingdom of the world as a citizen of the kingdom of God, you've got to know who you really are.

Once in Babylon, the full-court press to become Babylonian was applied to the boys from Jerusalem. And since their very names were actually statements of faith in the God of the Jews, those names had to go and be replaced by names that spoke of Babylonian deities. The boys were enrolled in a tuition-free, three-year program at the elite Babylonian University so that they might earn their MBA (their "Masters in Babylonian Administration"[13]). They were going to be taught the language of Babylon, but more than that, they were going to be immersed in the literature of Babylon. The goal was that they become enamored with the myths and stories and history of Babylon so that the book of Moses, the psalms of David, and the wisdom of Solomon would become a distant, nostalgic memory of an old life.

Babylon not only intended to educate them in the best school in the world; it intended to feed them in the finest restaurant in the world—no typical college cafeteria fare here. They were going to eat at the same white-linen-tablecloth restaurant at which the king ate every day. What sixteen- or seventeen-year-old boy would say no to that? We're about to meet one.

> But Daniel resolved that he would not defile himself with the king's food, or with the wine that he drank. . . . Then Daniel said to the steward whom the chief of the eunuchs had assigned over Daniel, Hananiah, Mishael, and Azariah, "Test your servants for ten days; let us be given vegetables to eat and water to drink." . . . So the steward took away their food and the wine they were to drink, and gave them vegetables. (Dan. 1:8, 11–12, 16)

Every day, as everybody else lined up at the lavish buffet and stuck their forks in filet, Daniel and his friends said, "I'll just have a salad." Why? Daniel and his friends were evidently willing to accept new names. They were evidently willing to learn the language and read the literature. But there is one thing they wouldn't do, one line they determined they would not cross. But, why this one? Why wouldn't they eat the king's food?

Is it because they were determined to eat a healthy, vegetarian diet or a diet according to Jewish food laws? Is it that this meat would have been offered to idols? Is it that they simply didn't want to cozy up to the table with the king? Well, we know from reading in Daniel 10 that eventually the time came when Daniel did eat meat and drink wine in the kingdom, so it doesn't seem to be about health or food laws (Dan. 10:3). And if it was about the food being offered to idols, the vegetables would have been offered to idols before being served too, so that doesn't seem to fit. Throughout the book we see that Daniel committed his life to serving the king, so it doesn't seem that sharing a meal with him would have been a big problem.

We don't know exactly why Daniel drew the line here, in regard to food. Perhaps it was because he knew that once you get a taste for the high life, it is difficult to do anything that might risk losing it. Perhaps Daniel recognized the message that was being sent at every mealtime: *the king's palace is the place to be; here's where the doors of opportunity are; taste the success; this is the fast track; enjoy.* Perhaps Daniel knew that if he embraced everything placed before him in Babylon, it wouldn't be long before his soul was consumed by it and he'd begin to think he simply had to have it and couldn't live without it. Perhaps Daniel recognized that he needed to set up for himself a daily reminder that Babylon was not his true home and that he belonged to another kingdom and another king.

The ways of the kingdom of the world are vividly illustrated here. The king did not pummel them with persecution, at least not yet. Instead, he opened up the doors of opportunity, seeking to intoxicate them with the splendors of life in his kingdom, hoping that these things will gradually erode their convictions and connections to Jerusalem. His desire was that they become so consumed with the good things the world offers that they would lose their sense of identity as citizens of a holy nation set apart to God, allowing obedience to God's law to become a relic, a cultural thing they looked back on but had grown beyond.

Some of us go through life evaluating the things the world presents to us and asking, is there anything wrong with it? And if we determine there is nothing inherently wrong with it, we freely dive in, embracing every primetime television show, every best-selling novel, every new self-help program, every clothing style, every must-have product and must-do adventure—while remaining willfully naïve about the erosive power these things have on our intimacy with Christ and our identity as one belonging to Christ. Daniel is showing us here that instead of asking, is there anything wrong with it? perhaps we should ask, will helping myself to this increase my sense of dependence upon and enjoyment of God, or does it have the potential to diminish my affections for him and connection to him? Could saying no to this help me to place a guard around my heart so that I will be reminded every day when I say no to it that I belong to another kingdom, that I serve another king?

You've Got to Know What Will Last

To live in the kingdom of the world, you've got to know who you really are, and, second, you've got to know what will really last. In Daniel 2 we find that King Nebuchadnezzar had experienced a dream, a disconcerting dream, and he was desperate to know what it meant. So Daniel called upon Yahweh, his true king, the revealer of mysteries, so that he might describe and interpret King Nebuchadnezzar's dream:

> You saw, O king, and behold, a great image. This image, mighty and of exceeding brightness, stood before you, and its appearance was frightening. The head of this image was of fine gold, its chest and arms of silver, its middle and thighs of bronze, its legs of iron, its feet partly of iron and partly of clay. As you looked, a stone was cut out by no human hand, and it struck the image on its feet of iron and clay, and broke them in pieces. Then the iron, the clay, the bronze, the silver, and the gold, all together were broken in pieces, and became like the chaff of the summer threshing floors; and the wind carried them away, so that not a trace of them could be found. (Dan. 2:31–35)

We could spend lots of time working our way through every part of the great image in the dream, identifying the ancient kingdom each stood for. But more important than determining the details is standing back to see the larger image and grasping the larger message. King Nebuchadnezzar was the head of gold in the image, while the chest, trunk, legs, and feet were kingdoms that would rise after his. The dream revealed one world power rising to dominance, only to be replaced by another and then another. Of course, this isn't just the course of ancient history; this is all of history, even our present reality. Human power and rule can be impressive for a time and do good things up to a point, but they are never permanent. Today's Babylonia was going to give way to tomorrow's Medo-Persian Empire. Yesterday's IBM gives way to Microsoft, which is overtaken by Apple. "Today's celebrities are tomorrow's obituaries."[14] The last big deal is replaced by today's big cheese only to be replaced by tomorrow's top dog. Daniel's interpretation in regard to the future of the kingdom of Babylon is as significant to us today as it was to Nebuchadnezzar that day:

> And in the days of those kings the God of heaven will set up a kingdom that shall never be destroyed, nor shall the kingdom be left to another people. It shall break in pieces all these kingdoms and bring them to an end, and it shall stand forever, just as you saw that a stone was cut from

a mountain by no human hand, and that it broke in pieces the iron, the bronze, the clay, the silver, and the gold. (Dan. 2:44–45)

God was revealing to Nebuchadnezzar, to Daniel, and to us what will last. He put impressive human power and progress into perspective for us. The final word of history does not lie with a new and improved version of man or anything he has made or accomplished. Rather, it lies with something radical: a rock not hewn by human hands. This stone is going to put an end to Babylon and all successive powers, while establishing a kingdom that will fill the whole earth and never be destroyed. For Daniel to live as a citizen of Jerusalem in Babylon meant that he had to put his hopes in this stone, in this kingdom that will last forever.

You've Got to Know Whom to Depend On

The next thing you've got to know to live in the kingdom of the world as a citizen of heaven is who to depend on. After interpreting Nebuchadnezzar's dream, Daniel was made chief prefect over all the wise men of Babylon, and his friends Shadrach, Meshach, and Abednego were put over the affairs of the province of Babylon. The kingdom of the world is not always hostile to citizens of the kingdom of God—especially when those citizens prove useful. But when their true allegiances are put to the test, the world can become very inhospitable indeed.

Daniel 3 sets the scene for this test of allegiance. Thousands of people from throughout the kingdom of Babylon gathered to dedicate the 90-foot golden image that Nebuchadnezzar had set up. He intended to unify all the conquered peoples from various lands, who worshiped all kinds of gods, by setting before them one object of worship—his own greatness. A world-class orchestra provided a soundtrack as all the people fell down to worship the golden image. Common sense must have screamed to Shadrach, Meshach, and Abednego, *Keep a low profile and live to fight another day. There's nothing to be gained by dying now when you have such valuable positions of influence. Just think of what a witness you'll be if you stay in the positions you're in. What matters is what's in your heart, so bowing with your body isn't a big deal.* Yet in the sea of people with faces to the ground, we see three men still standing, knowing full well a fire is being stoked for all who refuse to bow.

Evidently, once you've embraced God's revelation of all the world's powers turning to dust and blowing away in the wind, as they had in Daniel's interpretation of Nebuchadnezzar's dream, you're less impressed by the image you're being told to bow down to and the person telling you to do it. Evidently, when you know that you are part of a kingdom to come that cannot be destroyed, even by fire, you are less afraid of the fire. Your confidence in your true King and his ability to deliver you is far greater than your fear of the human king and his ability to destroy you. So they said to the king:

> O Nebuchadnezzar, we have no need to answer you in this matter. If this be so, our God whom we serve is able to deliver us from the burning fiery furnace, and he will deliver us out of your hand, O king. But if not, be it known to you, O king, that we will not serve your gods or worship the golden image that you have set up. (Dan. 3:16–18)

No defense. No apology. No pleading. They knew that King Nebuchadnezzar had no ultimate power; only God has that. They didn't know what God would do. But they trusted him. Their study of Babylonian literature hadn't erased what they knew from the Hebrew Scriptures—that they served a God who delivers his people, a God who had promised that the seed of the woman will crush the head of the seed of the Serpent. They were convinced he could be trusted to do right by them. So they were bound and thrown into the raging furnace.

> Then King Nebuchadnezzar was astonished and rose up in haste. He declared to his counselors, "Did we not cast three men bound into the fire?" They answered and said to the king, "True, O king." He answered and said, "But I see four men unbound, walking in the midst of the fire, and they are not hurt; and the appearance of the fourth is like a son of the gods." Then Nebuchadnezzar came near to the door of the burning fiery furnace; he declared, "Shadrach, Meshach, and Abednego, servants of the Most High God, come out, and come here!" Then Shadrach, Meshach, and Abednego came out from the fire. And the satraps, the prefects, the gov-

ernors, and the king's counselors gathered together and saw that the fire
had not had any power over the bodies of those men. The hair of their
heads was not singed, their cloaks were not harmed, and no smell of fire
had come upon them. (Dan. 3:24–27)

They weren't delivered *from* the fire. They were delivered *in* the fire.
There in the fire they experienced God's presence with them like never
before. Perhaps that's why the king had to command them to come
out. When we say no to the world and yes to God, the fire might actually be seven times hotter than we expected. But we can be sure that
in the midst of that fire, we will enjoy fellowship with Christ that we
wouldn't trade for anything.

In the heart of the first half of the book, chapters 4 and 5, we have
the accounts of what happened to the kings and kingdoms of Babylon
in Daniel's day. In chapter 4 we read that King Nebuchadnezzar had
had another dream, which Daniel interpreted to indicate that the king
would not only lose his power but also his rationality so that he would
behave like a wild animal. And that's exactly what happened.

Then in chapter 5 we read about the next and last king to rule over
ancient Babylon, Belshazzar, who had a vision of a human hand writing on the wall of his palace, revealing that God had numbered the
days of his kingdom, that he had been weighed in the balances and
found wanting, and that his kingdom would be divided and given to
the Medes and Persians. Here at the heart of the book of Daniel we have
the heart of Daniel's message: that human kings and kingdoms are not
ultimate and do not last.

When we next meet Daniel, he is no longer the newly exiled teen-
ager. He has become a wizened eighty- or ninety-year-old man and is
serving Darius, the Mede, who had become king. By the straightness of
his character, Daniel constantly revealed the crookedness of his col-
leagues, and they didn't appreciate that one bit. So they came up with
a plan to ruin him. They'd get the king to establish an ordinance, that
whoever makes petition to any god of man for thirty days, except to the
king, will be cast into the den of lions (Dan. 6:7). They knew well that
ever since Daniel turned down the king's food back in college, though

he had served the king and the country well, he had never truly come to depend on the king. He still depended on his God. As a citizen of Jerusalem, Daniel's heart was still set on the city of God. When Daniel heard about the ordinance and the waiting den of lions, we might expect to see him panic or go to the king and petition him to change his mind or organize a protest or simply make his faith a private matter. But he did none of those things:

> He went to his house where he had windows in his upper chamber open toward Jerusalem. He got down on his knees three times a day and prayed and gave thanks before his God, as he had done previously. (Dan. 6:10)

The next day Daniel was cast into the den of lions. You have to wonder if Darius had heard the story about Yahweh's deliverance of the three men in the fire years earlier, since when he went to the den the next morning, he said, "O Daniel, servant of the living God, has your God, whom you serve continually, been able to deliver you from the lions?" Sure enough, he heard a calm voice call back, saying, "O king, live forever! My God sent his angel and shut the lions' mouths, and they have not harmed me." (Dan. 6:20–22)

As a citizen of Jerusalem, Daniel refused to allow Babylon's intimidation tactics to detour him from his dependence upon God. And just as his friends experienced the protection and presence of God in the fire that threatened to consume them, Daniel enjoyed the protection and presence of God in the den of lions that threatened to consume him. And it begs the question: Can you see what threatens to consume you as you live your life in exile in Babylon? Is your allegiance to God so much a part of you that you cannot bow down to this world's ways? Is your dependence upon God such a daily part of life that you find it ridiculous to expect anything or anyone in this world to meet your needs?

This book of Daniel shows us how to live in Babylon as citizens of Jerusalem. And we are grateful for it, because we want to live that way. And yet, we have to admit, there's a problem. We want to be able to say no to the comforts of life for Christ's sake and be determined to keep ourselves pure. We want to have the courage to refuse to bow even if it means being thrown into the fire. We want to be so diligent in and so dependent on prayer that even the threat of being torn to shreds by a lion can't keep us from it. But we know we aren't that strong. We aren't that faithful. So what do we do with the book of Daniel? Are we supposed to read it and just try harder to be like Daniel and his friends?

You've Got to Know Who Lived This Way

Here is what happens when we shine the light of Christ on the book of Daniel. We see that there is one who did live this way. The King of heaven, the New Jerusalem, was sent into exile in the Babylon of this world. He knew who he really was, and what really lasts, and who to depend on. He resolved not to be defiled as he made his home in this world. And he did make his home in this world. Rather than dining at the king's table, he was known for eating with sinners and tax collectors. Yet he who resolved not to defile himself was defiled not by demands for his own worldly comforts, but by ours; not by his compromise to get ahead, but by ours. He was defiled so that you and I might be made pure and clean, so that we might one day dine at the true King's table and be satisfied forever.

Hundreds of years after Daniel, when Jesus read in Daniel's book about Nebuchanezzar's dream of the huge image made of gold, silver, bronze, iron, and clay, and about the stone "cut out by no human hand" that struck the image on its feet of iron and clay and broke them in pieces, Jesus saw himself. He called himself "the stone the builders rejected which has become the cornerstone," adding, "Everyone who falls on that stone will be broken to pieces, and when it falls on anyone, it will crush him" (Luke 20:17–18). So when we read in Daniel about this stone that struck the image becoming a great mountain and filling the whole earth, we recognize it as a description of how Jesus said his own kingdom will one day fill the whole earth.

Oh, how you and I would like to be so courageous, that when we see the whole world bow to the images of achievement in this world—business success, media stardom, sports greatness, mother-of-the-year, and yard-of-the-month—we would refuse to bow. We want to be like Shadrach, Meshach, and Abednego, so convinced that God's honor is worthy of our exclusive devotion, so clear that the things of the world do not deserve our allegiance. Yet we see ourselves bowing down, not standing firm, fearful of losing rather than confident in God's delivering. And this is why we need so much more than the example of Shadrach, Meshach, and Abednego. What we need is to be joined by faith to the one who was offered all the kingdoms of the world and their glory, the one to whom the Devil said, "All these I will give you, if you will fall down and worship me" (Matt. 4:9). Jesus refused to bow down, reserving his allegiance for God alone. And because he did not bow down, we can know that when judgment day comes, God will not look at us and see all our bowing down to human achievement. Instead, when he looks at us he will see us in Christ, who did not bow.

Because of Jesus, you and I don't have to be afraid of the fiery furnace. Because he went into the fire and did not emerge unscathed but was consumed by the fires of hell itself, we can be sure that even if we lose our lives for his cause, our resurrection day will come when we will emerge from death unscathed, unharmed, with no scent of fire.

Just as King Belshazzar saw the hand writing on the wall that he had been weighed and found wanting and that the days of his kingdom were numbered, so you and I deserve to have written on the walls of our lives: "Weighed and found wanting," "A failed kingdom unto herself," and "Her days are numbered." Yet instead, because we are joined to Christ, a nail-scarred hand has written across our lives, "Made worthy by the worth of Christ," "Co-heir of an eternal kingdom," and "Numbered among those whose lives will matter forever."

We look at Daniel's integrity, the one in whom "they could find no ground for complaint or any fault, because he was faithful, and no error or fault was found in him" (Dan. 6:4), and we know that the same could not be said of us. In fact, the hard truth is, if we were commanded not to pray for thirty days, it probably wouldn't make much difference in our lives because consistent prayer is just not that important in our lives.

Here is the good news of the gospel for all of us in whom fault can be found, all of us who have not persevered in prayer: there is one who spent entire nights in prayer, one who even now prays for us. He is the one about whom Pilate said, "I find no guilt in him" (John 19:4). It is his Spirit at work within us that gives us the desire and the power to live as "children of God without blemish in the midst of a crooked and twisted generation" (Phil. 2:15).

You've Got to Know How the Story Will End

There is one more thing we've got to know as we persevere as citizens of the kingdom of God living in the kingdom of the world. We've got to know how the story will end. Daniel was given a vision that enabled him to see into the distant future that we too need to see.

> As I looked,
>
> thrones were placed,
>   and the Ancient of Days took his seat;
> his clothing was white as snow,
>   and the hair of his head like pure wool;
> his throne was fiery flames;
>   its wheels were burning fire.
> A stream of fire issued
>   and came out from before him;
> a thousand thousands served him,
>   and ten thousand times ten thousand stood before him;
> the court sat in judgment,
>   and the books were opened. (Dan. 7:9–10)

Daniel saw the God of heaven seated on the throne of the universe, reigning in the kingdom that crushes every human kingdom. The thousand thousands who serve him do so gladly. In his blazing purity, he has the right to rule and the right to sit in judgment over every person, every king, and every kingdom that has ever been and will ever be.

Then we read that Daniel saw beasts whose "dominion was taken away, but their lives were prolonged for a season and a time" (Dan. 7:11–12). Here is Daniel, living in a world where kingdoms of the world growl and consume like beasts. And when he is given a vision of what is to come, he sees that the cruel forces at work in this world are not going to have their way forever. They will for "a season and a time." But their dominion will be taken away. For, lo, their doom is sure. But there is more that Daniel sees:

I saw in the night visions,

and behold, with the clouds of heaven
    there came one like a son of man,
and he came to the Ancient of Days
    and was presented before him.
And to him was given dominion
    and glory and a kingdom,
that all peoples, nations, and languages
    should serve him;
his dominion is an everlasting dominion,
    which shall not pass away,
and his kingdom one
    that shall not be destroyed. (Dan. 7:13–14)

Daniel saw the King who was going to come into the world from heaven, one "like a son of man." Throughout Jesus's ministry, his preferred way of referring to himself was "Son of Man." But, frankly, he did not appear to be anything like Daniel's description of the son of man. He looked less like a king and more like a servant. So the people of his day didn't really appreciate it when he referred to himself as "the Son of Man," as he did before the high priest the night before he was crucified.

> The high priest said to him, "I adjure you by the living God, tell us if you are the Christ, the Son of God." Jesus said to him, "You have said so. But I tell you, from now on you will see the Son of Man seated at the right hand of Power and coming on the clouds of heaven. (Matt. 26:63–64)

Jesus was speaking to men who knew what Daniel had written about a son of man who would come. So did these religious leaders bow to him? Did they honor him as King? No, they mocked him as king. Matthew writes: "They stripped him and put a scarlet robe on him, and twisting together a crown of thorns, they put it on his head and put a reed in his right hand. And kneeling before him, they mocked him, saying, 'Hail, King of the Jews!' And they spit on him and took the reed and struck him on the head" (Matt. 27:28–30).

Jesus was not delivered from the flames of judgment. When Jesus was thrown into the den, God sent no angel to shut the mouth of the roaring lion who seeks to devour. Jesus was consumed by the flames; he was consumed by the lion. But just as he promised, after three days he emerged from the flames of death triumphant, with no smell of death lingering on him. Just as a stone was put over the lion's den when Daniel was put in it, so a stone was placed over the tomb where Jesus was buried. But the stone was rolled away, and Jesus emerged having been given all authority in heaven and on earth (Matt. 28:18).

You've got to know how the story is going to end. One day, on a day no one in the kingdom of the world expects, the kingdom of heaven is going to come down. The Son of Man is going to come in glory and power. The stone who has become the cornerstone will be the foundation of the New Jerusalem, the eternal city of God. The kingdom of the world will become the kingdom of our Lord and of his Christ, and he shall reign forever and ever (Rev. 11:15).

Looking Forward

Fallen, Fallen Is Babylon!

In the book of Daniel we read about Babylon's defeat of Jerusalem. And when we come to the end of the Bible, in the book of Revelation, we read about the final defeat of Babylon. As John wrote down the vision he was given of the final defeat of Babylon, the Emperor Domitian was on the Roman throne demanding to be addressed as "lord and god," just as the Babylonian kings Daniel served had demanded to be treated as gods. Exiled on the Island of Patmos, John was given the same vision that had been given to Daniel centuries before when he was exiled in Babylon. Daniel was given a vision of the future so that the people of his day would know that human powers that rebel against God and make life miserable in this world will ultimately fail and that the stone not made with human hands will ultimately crush all human kingdoms. Likewise, John was given the same vision so that the people in his day and our day would put our hopes in God's revelation that one day the city of man and its ways will be defeated for good.

John saw the proud city of man come to a disastrous end, writing, "Fallen, fallen is Babylon the great!" (Rev. 18:2). But that is not all he saw:

> I saw the holy city, new Jerusalem, coming down out of heaven from God, prepared as a bride adorned for her husband. And I heard a loud voice from the throne saying, "Behold, the dwelling place of God is with man. He will dwell with them, and they will be his people, and God himself will be with them as their God." (Rev. 21:1–3)

Finally, exile will be over. All those who have overcome the allures of Babylon, who have built their lives on the rock—Jesus himself—putting their faith in what he accomplished on the cross rather than on what they could accomplish themselves, will be welcomed into the New Jerusalem. We'll finally be at home, dining at the king's table, living joyfully under the rule of our true king. Babylon itself will have been thrown into the fiery furnace, and the lion who prowled around seeking whom he might devour will himself be devoured.

Daniel

Getting the Discussion Going

1. What kind of pressures does the world put on us in modern-day life to be citizens of the kingdom of the world?

Getting to the Heart of It

2. Daniel drew a line that he would not cross in his resolve not to be defiled by the world. In our day Christians draw lines in different places. And some really don't draw any lines at all. What difference do you think it makes if we ask, Is this wise? rather than, Is this right or wrong?

3. Daniel 2 and 7 are similar in what they show of dreams and visions of the rise and fall of human kingdoms and the promised coming of a kingdom that will bring an end to every human kingdom. If you had been living in exile in Babylon in Daniel's day and heard about these dreams and visions and Daniel's interpretations of them, how do you think it would have impacted you?

4. Just as Daniel 2 and 7 are parallel, so are Daniel 3 and 6—one telling the story of Shadrach, Meshach, and Abednego being put in the fiery furnace, and the other telling the story of Daniel's being put in the den of lions. Both stories put the faith of the men as well as the deliverance

of God on display. What did they know that served as the foundation for their faith and confidence in God's deliverance?

5. When we read the stories of God's delivering them from the furnace and from the lion's den, we can't help but also think about the Christians who were later killed by lions in the Roman Colosseum, as well as Christians today who are tortured and killed for their faith in various parts of the world. How do we reconcile the stories of deliverance with the reality that God does not always seem to deliver his saints from harm?

6. How does the book of Daniel help us to understand more clearly who Christ is and what he came to do?

Getting Personal

7. The examples that Daniel, Shadrach, Meshach, and Abednego set before us as citizens of Jerusalem living in exile in Babylon are challenging. What are some of the ways their examples challenge you personally?

Getting How It Fits into the Big Picture

8. If you had only the scroll or book of Daniel but not the rest of the Bible, what would you know about what God is doing in the world and how he is going to do it?

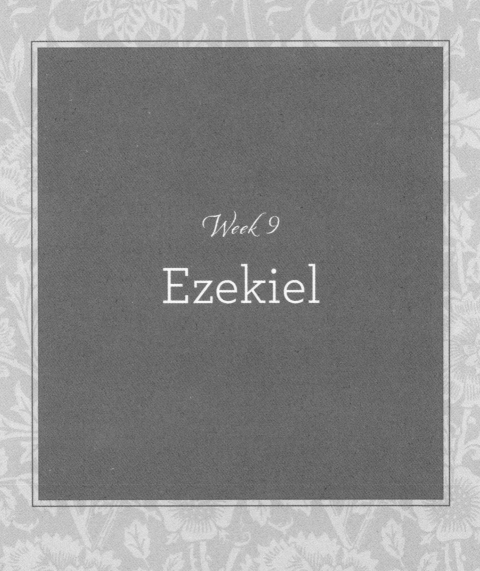

Week 9

Ezekiel

Ezekiel

Up to this point in our study we've heard from prophets who prophesied in the northern kingdom of Israel prior to their exile to Assyria, including Jonah and Hosea, and from prophets who prophesied to the southern kingdom of Judah long before and then right before they were taken into exile, including Micah, Isaiah, Habakkuk, and Jeremiah. Last week we studied Daniel who prophesied to exiles living in Babylon. This week we study another prophet who prophesied to God's people living in exile, not inside the city of Babylon, where Daniel was, but just outside the city in what could be described as a refugee camp where ten thousand exiles from Judah were taken to live.

1. Read through Ezekiel's first vision, found in Ezekiel 1, and note a few details (not necessarily every detail) about each of the following:

The storm (v. 4):

The four living creatures (vv. 5–14):

The wheels (vv. 15–21):

The expanse (vv. 22–25):

The throne (vv. 26–28):

2. In verse 28 we're told that what Ezekiel has seen is "the likeness of the glory of the LORD." If we look back at the previous verses, we see the word "likeness" is used ten times in the chapter. What do you think this might communicate about Ezekiel's description of what he saw?

3. Ezekiel 4–24 is primarily oracles preached about the judgment on Jerusalem. In the midst of these chapters Ezekiel has another vision that reveals how God views what is taking place in Jerusalem. List several things that Ezekiel saw in and around the temple, according to chapter 8.

4. Ezekiel 9 describes Ezekiel's vision of the judgment that will come down on all in Jerusalem except for a small remnant of repentant people who will be saved. Then, in chapter 10, the glory of God, which Ezekiel saw in his earlier vision, is on the move. In what way does the glory of God move in 10:18–19 and 11:23?

5. Though the people of Judah living in exile saw themselves as far removed from God's presence, which had earlier been with them in the temple in Jerusalem, what reality is revealed to Ezekiel in 11:16?

6. Ezekiel 25–33 contains a series of sermons preached throughout the three years of Babylon's siege of Jerusalem, with Ezekiel stressing that the surrounding nations will be judged in the way Judah is being judged. According to 33:21, how did the siege of Jerusalem end, and how do you think this impacted the exiles, who had been longing to go home to Jerusalem for twelve years?

7. Up to this point, Ezekiel's message has not really communicated any hope. But as soon as he hears Jerusalem has fallen, he begins to preach a message of hope, assuring the people that although the exile would

not be as temporary as they had originally thought, it would come to an end. What hope is held out to the exiles in the following passages?

34:11–16, 23–24

36:24–32

36:33–38

37:1–14

37:24–28

8. We've seen that God has promised a new king, a new heart, a new spirit, a new land, and a new life to his faithful remnant. Now, in Ezekiel 40–48, God promises through his prophet Ezekiel a new temple in which the people will enjoy a new experience of God's presence. In previous visions Ezekiel had seen the glory of God in the Jerusalem temple, and then he saw the glory of God depart from the Jerusalem temple. Now he sees the glory of God return to a new temple that far supersedes the old Jerusalem temple. What is the first thing we learn in Ezekiel 40:2 about this new temple?

9. In Ezekiel 47:1–12, the new temple is described as less like a city and more like something else. What does the description of the temple here remind you of? (You might also refer back to Ezekiel 36:35.)

10. Ezekiel 40–42 details the perfectly square structure of the new temple. Then we come to the most important thing about the garden-like city in the shape of a temple in 43:1–9, which is reiterated in 48:35.[15] What is it?

11. What does Hebrews 8:1–5 reveal to us about the Old Testament tabernacle and temple?

12. What do we learn from Jesus in the following verses about the new temple Ezekiel saw?

Matthew 12:6

John 2:13–22

13. What do the following verses reveal about where or what form this new temple takes in the present?

1 Corinthians 3:16–17

Ephesians 2:19–22

14. Revelation 21:1–22:5 describes the new heaven and the new earth. Read through this passage and list as many examples as you'd like of aspects of the new heaven and the new earth that reflect a garden, a city, and the temple (keeping in mind that a whole book could be written on this!).

Teaching Chapter

The House That Built Me

Recently I had one of those birthdays that ends in a zero, and I told David that, to celebrate, I wanted to invite over a few musical friends and have my own personal songwriter night. It's a very Nashville thing—songwriters in the round, singing songs they have written. Our version was slightly different from the norm. One of our friends quoted Romans 8 from memory and sang an old hymn. Another friend changed the words to the Frank Sinatra song "Nancy with the Laughing Face" to make them about me (and by the way, how did I live this many years on the planet without knowing there was a song that had "Nancy" in the title?). Our friend Tom Douglas sang the song that he co-wrote with Allen Shamblin that won the CMA and ACM Song of the Year Award in 2010, "The House That Built Me." Let me just say: Best. Birthday Party. Ever.

Tom's song, "The House That Built Me," tells the story of someone who visits the house she grew up in, hoping that she can get back in touch with the person she was when she lived there, the person she has somehow lost along the way of life in this world. Her hope is that if she can just spend some time in this house, remembering who she was brought up to be and who she wanted to be, then perhaps she will begin to experience healing in the broken places of her life.

I wonder if you ever feel this way—if you ever find yourself living with the nagging sense of having veered off course somewhere along the way in becoming the person you had hoped to be, living out the kind of life you had hoped to live. I wonder if you ever sense a longing to find the place where the brokenness inside you could find healing.

The Bible is the story of the house that God built, the house he is building, and as we take it in, we realize that it is, in fact, the house that has made us who we are, the only house where we will ever truly be at home, the only place where we can find the healing we long for, the house in which God himself intends to live with us forever. God created us to live in a sanctuary with him. The Bible tells the story of how we lost ourselves as we were meant to be and therefore lost the home we were meant to have with him. It tells us the story of what God is doing so that we might, once again, find ourselves, find healing, find him—in the house that he has built and is building.

To grasp this story, we have to go back to the beginning, when God began building the house he intends to live in with his people. The building process began when, "in the beginning, God created the heavens and the earth" (Gen. 1:1). God furnished his home with colorful blooming plants and nourished it with babbling streams and flooded it with radiant light shining out of blue sky. He came down in the cool of the day to walk with those he had made to live with him there. They were supposed to be fruitful and multiply and expand the borders of this garden sanctuary so that eventually the whole earth would become a sacred space where God lived among those made in his image, reflecting his glory. This sanctuary was full of God's glory and goodness. That's what makes it hard to understand how Eve could fall for the Serpent's suggestion that God was withholding something good from her and Adam. But she did. Adam and Eve proved to be like rebellious teenagers in God's house of Eden and were kicked out of the house.

God has been at work ever since to bring those he loves back in to what we might call "Eden 2.0," a vast and more populated version in which nothing evil or unclean will ever enter to spoil it. He began by calling a people to himself and leading them to a land where he intended to come down and live among them. He gave them detailed instructions for building the house that he intended to live in. We read about it first in Exodus where the Lord told Moses, "Let them make me a sanctuary, that I may dwell in their midst. Exactly as I show you concerning the pattern of the tabernacle, and of all its furniture, so you shall make it" (Ex. 25:8–9). Why was following the pattern so important? Because the mobile tabernacle and the immobile temple that followed it were designed to point both backward and forward. The writer of Hebrews says they were "copies of the true things"(9:24) and "a shadow of the good things to come" (10:1). If we look closely at the design, it becomes obvious what the tabernacle and the temple were copies or shadows of. They were a little piece of the paradise of Eden. More than that, they were like architectural models of Eden 2.0, the new heaven and the new earth.

In 1 Kings 6 and 2 Chronicles 3 we read about the house of the Lord that Solomon built in Jerusalem, with gourds and open flowers carved into the cedar walls; pomegranates carved in the latticework; two cherubim made of wood with wings spread out seemingly on guard over the Most Holy Place; a basin made to look like a lily; lampstands made to look like trees with branches; and the veil woven with blue, purple, and crimson fabrics; all of it overlaid with sparkling gold. The psalmist described it, saying, "He built his sanctuary like the high heavens, like the earth, which he has founded forever" (Ps. 78:69). When you walked into the temple it took you back—back to the beauty of the house God had built so long ago, that initial outpost of heaven, the garden of Eden. But it also pointed forward to something God is going to do in the future to make it possible for his people to be at home with him again, a day when heaven will come down to earth so that earth will become heaven.

The Glory Descends

When Solomon had completed the temple we read:

> A cloud filled the house of the LORD, so that the priests could not stand to minister because of the cloud, for the glory of the LORD filled the house of the LORD. (1 Kings 8:10–11)

All the people of Israel saw fire come down and the visible presence of God rest on and fill the temple. The temple in Jerusalem, specifically the Most Holy Place in the temple, became the habitation of heaven on earth, an extension of God's throne room. Its perfectly cubed dimensions reflected the perfection of heaven and the God who dwells there, and its shimmering gold overlay reflected the brightness and glory of heaven and radiated into every nook and cranny of the place.

But when we open up the book of the prophet Ezekiel, the people of God were finding no comfort that God dwells in the Most Holy Place of the temple in Jerusalem. Ezekiel and ten thousand inhabitants of Judah had been taken nine hundred miles away from Jerusalem to live in a refugee camp outside the city of Babylon, adjacent to a drainage ditch called the Chebar canal. Many thought this would be just a brief stint away from home, while others were convinced that God had utterly abandoned them there. Some so-called prophets had advised the refugees not to unpack, saying that they'd be back in Jerusalem before they knew it. Yet Jeremiah the prophet, back in Jerusalem, had prophesied that the exile would last for seventy years, and then God would bring them back.

Ezekiel was the son of a priest and had been raised in the days of Josiah, the king who rediscovered the Book of the Law in the temple and brought about tremendous reforms. When Ezekiel was seventeen, he saw Nebuchadnezzar come over the horizon and take many of Jerusalem's brightest and best into captivity in Babylon, including his friends Daniel, Hananiah, Mishael, and Azariah. When Ezekiel was twenty-five, the king of Jerusalem rebelled against Babylon's domination, and the armies came again, this time taking Ezekiel and ten thousand other Jews, including King Jehoiachin, to a refugee camp outside Babylon. Up to the time he was taken from Jerusalem at the age of twenty-five, Ezekiel had spent his life preparing to be a priest in the temple of Jerusalem.

When we meet Ezekiel, he too was having a birthday that ends in a zero. He was thirty. Turning thirty meant something significant to Ezekiel. It was the age at which he would have begun serving in the temple as a priest. So this could not have been a very happy birthday. It was supposed to have been a birthday celebration, graduation party, and ordination ceremony rolled into one, but those plans, that dream, is or was long gone. His life was not turning out at all like he had hoped.

Ezekiel must have longed to go back to Jerusalem, back to the temple, back to the house that had built and shaped him to be who he was. But we're going to see that in this hard place, God revealed something to Ezekiel that changed everything about his longing for home. In fact, it changed everything that he understood about where home is and what makes it home. And if you feel so far away from being where you wanted to be in life, so far away from being all you thought God intended for you to be, perhaps you need to see what Ezekiel saw.

> In the thirtieth year, in the fourth month, on the fifth day of the month, as I was among the exiles by the Chebar canal, the heavens were opened, and I saw visions of God. On the fifth day of the month (it was the fifth year of the exile of King Jehoiachin), the word of the LORD came to Ezekiel the priest, the son of Buzi, in the land of the Chaldeans by the Chebar canal, and the hand of the LORD was upon him there. (Ezek. 1:1–3)

God met this displaced, disappointed man and gave him something far better than a lifetime of lighting candles and offering sacrifices at the temple in Jerusalem. God showed Ezekiel something that very few people in the Old Testament era ever got a glimpse of: God pulled back the curtain of heaven so that Ezekiel could see the glory of God. When we feel disoriented and disillusioned, what we need most is for God to lift our eyes from the difficulties of this life to see into the reality of where he is and who he is and what he is doing. That's what Ezekiel saw in this first vision:

> As I looked, behold, a stormy wind came out of the north, and a great cloud, with brightness around it, and fire flashing forth continually, and in the midst of the fire, as it were gleaming metal. And from the midst of it came the likeness of four living creatures. And this was their appearance: they had a human likeness, but each had four faces, and each of them had four wings. (Ezek. 1:4–6)

Ezekiel saw four living creatures that represent the whole created order:

> Now as I looked at the living creatures, I saw a wheel on the earth beside the living creatures, one for each of the four of them. . . . And . . . their appearance and construction being as it were a wheel within a wheel.

> When they went, they went in any of their four directions without turn-
> ing as they went. (Ezek.1:15–17)

This is unusual. Under the living creatures are wheels within wheels.
Think of castors on the bottom of an ottoman so that the wheels can
easily move in any direction. As he continues, notice how many times
Ezekiel uses the term "the likeness of." He seems to be struggling to
find words to describe something that is beyond words—the glory of
God—which descended to dwell in Jerusalem:

> Over the heads of the living creatures there was the likeness of an expanse,
> shining like awe-inspiring crystal, spread out above their heads. . . . And
> above the expanse over their heads there was the likeness of a throne, in
> appearance like sapphire; and seated above the likeness of a throne was
> a likeness with a human appearance. . . . Such was the appearance of the
> likeness of the glory of the LORD. (Ezek. 1:22, 26, 28)

It is as if the wings of the living creatures are jointly upholding an
expansive platform that looks like it is made of sparkling crystal on
which the throne of God sits. It reminds us of Isaiah's vision of the Lord
"high and lifted up" (Isa. 6:1), except that here the glory of God is not
static in the temple; it's dynamic. It's on the move. The Israelites saw
God as settled and perhaps confined to their temple in Jerusalem. But
these wheels, which are able to move in any direction, reveal that there
is no place that God cannot go. The fact that the wheels are covered
with eyes tells us that there is nothing that he cannot see. Ezekiel has
seen that God's presence among his people is not confined to an architectural structure in Jerusalem.

The Glory Departs

It is fourteen months later when Ezekiel was given another vision
of the glory of God, which is recorded in chapters 8–11. Through
this vision Ezekiel was given a tour of what was happening back
in Jerusalem at the temple complex. He was shown the idol of the
Canaanite goddess Asherah that stood at the north gate (8:5), seventy Israelite elders offering incense to idols carved into the walls

in a secret chamber in the outer courts of the temple where they thought the Lord could not see them (8:7–13), and women weeping for Tammuz in a Babylonian fertility ritual (8:14). He saw into the inner court of the temple itself where twenty-five men were prostrating themselves toward the east, worshiping the sun (8:16). He saw every kind of person worshiping every kind of false god, right in front of God's face. God had seen it all, and evidently he was ready to move out of his house:

> And the glory of the LORD went up from the cherub to the threshold of the house, and the house was filled with the cloud, and the court was filled with the brightness of the glory of the LORD. (Ezek. 10:4)

The glory of the Lord has moved to the threshold of the temple. When we are in our home and walk to the threshold, what are we doing? We're leaving. To Ezekiel, who loved the house of the Lord in Jerusalem, this must have been horrifying. He saw the glory of God moving toward the door to leave the temple he loved.

> Then the glory of the LORD went out from the threshold of the house, and stood over the cherubim. And the cherubim lifted up their wings and mounted up from the earth before my eyes as they went out, with the wheels beside them. And they stood at the entrance of the east gate of the house of the LORD, and the glory of the God of Israel was over them. (Ezek. 10:18–19)

Ezekiel seems to sense that the glory of the Lord is departing the temple haltingly, reluctantly making its way from the threshold of the temple to the east gate of the city.

> Then the cherubim lifted up their wings, with the wheels beside them, and the glory of the God of Israel was over them. And the glory of the LORD went up from the midst of the city and stood on the mountain that is on the east side of the city. (Ezek. 11:22–23)

The glory of the Lord has not just left the temple; it has left the city heading east. Where is it going?

> Thus says the Lord GOD: Though I removed them far off among the
> nations, and though I scattered them among the countries, yet I have been
> a sanctuary to them for a while in the countries where they have gone.
> (Ezek. 11:16)

Perhaps Ezekiel had been thinking that God was abandoning his
people, but, in fact, God was headed east to where his people were
living by the Chebar canal. God was going into exile with his people.
He was moving the focus of his redeeming plan of grace away from
Jerusalem, where his people had turned from God to idols, and toward
the faithful remnant in exile.

> "Thus says the Lord GOD: I will gather you from the peoples and assemble
> you out of the countries where you have been scattered, and I will give
> you the land of Israel." And when they come there, they will remove from
> it all its detestable things and all its abominations. And I will give them
> one heart, and a new spirit I will put within them. I will remove the heart
> of stone from their flesh and give them a heart of flesh, that they may
> walk in my statutes and keep my rules and obey them. And they shall be
> my people, and I will be their GOD. (Ezek. 11:17–20)

"They shall be my people, and I will be their God." We've heard this
before. This was the reality Adam and Eve enjoyed in the garden before
the fall. This is what God had promised to Abraham. This was the goal
of the exodus out of Egypt. And now we see it is still what God is working toward, what he is bringing about. His people may be far from
home, but they are not forgotten, not abandoned. God intends to be a
sanctuary, a home for them, right there by the Chebar canal. And he is
not going to leave them there forever. One day they are going to come
back to Jerusalem, and they will be changed people when they come
back. The idolatry that has taken over in Jerusalem will be cleansed
away and gone for good.

So Ezekiel, who once thought that his ministry was going nowhere
because he wasn't in Jerusalem to serve in the temple, found out that
the saving purposes of God were not in Jerusalem but right there among
the exiles by the Chebar canal in Babylon. We can never think that
God's saving purposes for us are confined to what we had in mind as

Plan A for our lives. If you belong to him, you can be sure that his saving purposes are at work in you wherever your life and circumstances and his sovereign plans for you have taken you.

In their ninth year in exile, Ezekiel learned that the city of Jerusalem was under siege. Then three years later he received the news that Nebuchadnezzar's armies had succeeded in demolishing Jerusalem. Imagine the distress of the exiles when they got this news. The home they loved and were longing to return to had been turned into a desolation and a waste (Ezek. 33:21, 29). There was no more Jerusalem to go back to, no temple to worship in if they did go back. But at this low point, when it seemed there was no more reason to hope, Ezekiel was given yet another vision of God's glory. He had seen God's glory descend, he had seen it depart, and then he was given a vision of a time in the future when the glory of God would return to the temple in Jerusalem.

The Glory Returns

Ezekiel was fifty years old when he was given this vision of God's glory (which, I would have to say, would have made it an even better birthday party than having your own personal songwriter night).

> In the fourteenth year after the city was struck down, on that very day, the hand of the LORD was upon me, and he brought me to the city. In visions of God he brought me to the land of Israel, and set me down on a very high mountain, on which was a structure like a city to the south. (Ezek. 40:1–2)

"A structure like a city"—this was a vision of a new temple, yet it was more like a city. Over chapters 40–43, the dimensions of this temple are given not in feet or inches but in miles. Clearly this temple is going to be on a whole new scale compared to the former temple in Jerusalem.

> And behold, the glory of the God of Israel was coming from the east. And the sound of his coming was like the sound of many waters, and the earth shone with his glory. And the vision I saw was just like the vision that I had seen when he came to destroy the city, and just like the vision that I had seen by the Chebar canal. And I fell on my face. As the glory of the

LORD entered the temple by the gate facing east, the Spirit lifted me up
and brought me into the inner court; and behold, the glory of the LORD
filled the temple. (Ezek. 43:2–5)

In his vision Ezekiel is on a mountain overlooking Jerusalem,
where a massive new temple is taking shape that envelops not just the
old temple complex but the entire city. Then he looks up, and arriving
from the east, from the direction of the exiles in Babylon, is the tangible, visible glory of God, coming to inhabit this new temple.

Throughout chapters 43–46 we read about the altar, the priests,
the feasts and festivals, and the offerings and sacrifices in this new
temple, all of which sound familiar. Then we come to chapter 47 and
find something very different about this temple compared to the previous temple in Jerusalem. Water is flowing out of this temple, and as it
flows, it becomes ankle-deep and then knee-deep and then waist-deep
and finally a river that can't be crossed. Everywhere the river flows
becomes fresh and alive again. It is transforming the world as the blessing of God pours out from this new temple to the ends of the earth. On
the bank of the river are trees. "Their leaves will not wither, nor their
fruit fail, but they will bear fresh fruit every month, because the water
for them flows from the sanctuary. Their fruit will be for food, and their
leaves for healing" (Ezek. 47:12). It's beginning to sound like the garden of Eden all over again, except even better. Surely this is Eden 2.0.
Ezekiel's vision ends by telling us the name of this garden-like city that
is shaped like a temple:

> And the name of the city from that time on shall be, The LORD Is There.
> (Ezek. 48:35)

What will make this city home for all of its true citizens is that the person they love with all their heart, soul, mind, and strength lives there.
It reminds me of something I realized a while ago when someone asked
me to go on a ministry trip overseas that would last two weeks. I had
to tell her that the only way I'd go for that length of time was if David
came with me. I can be gone from my home in Nashville for a long time
if David is with me, because wherever we are together is home. It is that

sense of rest, that same sense of God's people finally being at home, that Ezekiel sees in his vision—this new city, this new temple, will be home because the one they love the most will be there. They will see him and know him like never before.

Ezekiel saw the glory of God descend, he saw it depart, and then he saw a vision of the day when the glory of God will return. But when will that be? Yes, the exiles later returned to Jerusalem and rebuilt a temple of sorts. But they certainly didn't try to build it to the specifications given by Ezekiel, as if they could. Never again did they see the glory of God descend on the temple in Jerusalem like it had in Solomon's day. But the glory of God did descend.

In John we read, "The Word became flesh and dwelt among us, and we have seen his glory, glory as of the only Son from the Father, full of grace and truth" (John 1:14). Once again the glory of God descended to dwell (or, to use John's actual Greek word, it "tabernacled") among his people, this time not in the form of a cloud and fire but in flesh and blood. Jesus is the "radiance of the glory of God" (Heb. 1:3). The glory of God stepped down from the throne to confine himself to a virgin's womb. Instead of the cherubim of heaven gazing upward at the glory, they gazed downward from heaven, staggered that the glory shared with the Father before the world existed should be wrapped in swaddling cloths lying in a manger.

The glory of God came to the temple in Jerusalem. When Jesus was just twelve years old, he recognized the temple as the house that built him, and he lingered there to discuss the Scriptures with the teachers, saying to his parents, "Did you not know that I must be in my Father's house?" (Luke 2:49). Jesus taught in the temple and healed in the temple and drove out the money-changers from the temple. When the Jews questioned his authority for doing so, he said, "Destroy this temple, and in three days I will raise it up." John writes that "he was speaking about the temple of his body. When therefore he was raised from the dead, his disciples remembered that he had said this, and *they believed the Scripture* and the word that Jesus had spoken" (John 2:19, 21–22).

When John writes that they "believed the Scripture," he likely means that they believed Ezekiel 40–48. Finally they could see that the new temple Ezekiel had seen in a vision had come in the person of Jesus Christ, the true temple.

But the presence of the glory of God, the true temple, was not wanted in the temple in Jerusalem. So the glory that descended to dwell there became the glory that departed, leaving not on a wheeled platform but carrying a wooden cross. The glory departed the temple going beyond the threshold and outside the gate of the city. There, the Lord of glory was crucified on a cross. But in three days, the true Temple was raised up. When this temple was raised, it wasn't an architectural wonder; it was a resurrection miracle. Forty days later the glory of God in the person of the risen Christ went to a mountain on the east of the city, the very place where Ezekiel had seen the glory departing the city (Ezek. 11:23). There, Jesus was lifted up, and a cloud took him out of sight. The glory departed. But an angel said he will come back the same way that he went into heaven (Acts 1:9–10). The glory will return.

When Christ rose from the grave, the new temple as part of the new creation was inaugurated, the temple that all of us who are in Christ are a part of as living stones. We are also priests serving in the holy place as "lampstands," shining the light of God's presence throughout the world, calling all people everywhere to worship him. And the day is coming when the glory of God will return, and the whole creation will have become God's sanctuary, the new temple. That's when we'll truly be at home. That is where all history is headed. We won't just see it in a vision as Ezekiel did. We'll see it with our eyes. Paul writes: "For the Lord himself will descend from heaven" (1 Thess. 4:16). The glory of God will return to make this earth his forever home.

But don't think that you have to wait until some time in the future to begin enjoying all that awaits us in this garden-like city in the shape of a temple that Ezekiel wrote about. You can start to drink now of the river that flows from the temple by coming to Jesus and drinking of him, allowing him to bring you to life as he satisfies your soul. You can start now to eat of the fruit of the tree of life and experience the healing of its leaves. This is how that brokenness inside you begins to heal—as you abide in Christ and his words abide in you, and he begins his healing work in the parts of your life that are diseased by sin, a healing work that begins now and will be completed on the day you enter into his presence.

God is even now building his new temple, not with limestone hewn from quarries in the Middle East but with living stones, the lives of ordinary believers like you and me. Peter writes that we are living stones that are being built up as a spiritual house (1 Pet. 2:5). And Paul writes:

> You are fellow citizens with the saints and members of the household of God, built on the foundation of the apostles and prophets, Christ Jesus himself being the cornerstone, in whom the whole structure, being joined together, grows into a holy temple in the Lord. In him you also are being built together into a dwelling place for God by the Spirit. (Eph. 2:19–22)

Jesus himself is the new temple. We as individual believers are temples of the Holy Spirit (1 Cor. 6:19). We as the church are being built into the new temple, a dwelling place for God by the Spirit. And one day we will live in the new temple that Ezekiel saw in his vision. On that day, when heaven comes to earth, the entire earth will become his sanctuary. So as we make our home in the house God is building, we discover that the house that built us is not just a nostalgic memory in our past but the glorious promise of our future. It's not something we have to build for ourselves but something that is being built for us, even in us. Our longing for this home leads us to pray with the psalmist:

> One thing have I asked of the LORD,
>   that will I seek after:
> that I may dwell in the house of the LORD
>   all the days of my life,
> to gaze upon the beauty of the LORD
>   and to inquire in his temple. (Ps. 27:4)

Come home to the house that built you. Come and find rest and healing in the garden. Come and put down your roots in the city of God called "The LORD Is There."

Looking Forward

No Temple in the City

When God placed Adam and Eve in the garden of Eden and told them to "be fruitful and multiply and fill the earth and subdue it" (Gen. 1:28), it was God's intention that the whole earth become a sacred space where God lives among those made in his image, reflecting his glory. Adam was supposed to widen the boundaries of the garden into the inhospitable outer spaces so that the garden of Eden would eventually cover the entire earth. But Adam failed. So God sent the second Adam, Jesus. The second Adam is, even now, expanding the borders of God's sanctuary. As his gospel goes out by his Spirit, remaking men and women into his image, the glory of God is spreading to every corner of the earth.

When we come to the end of the Bible, the book of Revelation, we discover that the entire recreated cosmos, and not a man-made building on a small patch of earth, will be the physical temple in which God's glory will dwell with his people forever. John writes:

> And I saw no temple in the city, for its temple is the Lord God the Almighty and the Lamb. And the city has no need of sun or moon to shine on it, for the glory of God gives it light, and its lamp is the Lamb. (Rev. 21:22–23)

There is no architectural temple in this city, but there is a temple. God's glorious presence makes this city a temple. Unlike in Ezekiel's day, God's glory won't be confined to the perfectly cubed Most Holy Place. It will permeate all of creation. The priests who serve in this temple will not be limited to a small number from a certain tribe who can enter the Most Holy Place only once a year. All who live there will be priests.

> The throne of God and of the Lamb will be in it, and his servants will worship him. They will see his face, and his name will be on their foreheads. (Rev. 22:3–4)

Just as the priests in the Old Testament temple wore headpieces that said, "Holy to the Lord," so the Lord's name will be on our foreheads. We will no longer need the lampstand that stood in the Old

Testament temple, because the Lord's very presence will illumine the new temple.

At the end of history God is going to come down from the invisible heavenly dimension, and the visible new heaven and new earth will be filled with the glory of the Lord so that the name of the city that covers the earth will be "The LORD Is There."

Discussion Guide

Ezekiel

Getting the Discussion Going

1. If we think of ourselves as sons and daughters of Adam and Eve, we realize that we all have a longing to get back to the house that built us—the home we once enjoyed in the garden of Eden. How do you think that life as it once was in the garden of Eden helps to explain the sense of disappointment we have with life in this world and how our lives have gone?

Getting to the Heart of It

2. If we consider that the garden of Eden was the first temple or sanctuary, what echoes of Eden do we find in the design and function of the Old Testament tabernacle and temple?

3. Let's consider Ezekiel's first vision of the glory of God found in Ezekiel 1. Imagine you were with Ezekiel as an exile from Jerusalem. What do you think you would have been able to learn from that unusual vision?

4. When news reached the exiles in Babylon that Jerusalem had fallen, it must have been a very distressing time. That's when Ezekiel began to prophesy of the new things God was going to do, which we saw briefly

in the Personal Bible Study concerning Ezekiel 34–37. Let's work our way through those passages to consider not only why these promises would be good news to the exiles but also how and when these promises have been, are being, or will be fulfilled.

5. Where or what or who is the temple now, and what are the implications of that?

6. In the final question of the Personal Bible Study, we were asked to read through Revelation 21:1–22:5, noting how the new heaven and the new earth are presented to us as a garden-like city in the shape of a temple. What are some of the things you discovered?

Getting Personal

7. God's covenant promise throughout the Bible is that he will be our God and we will be his people. Over and over he announces his intention to dwell with his people. Does that sound like a good thing to you? Why or why not? What do you think could help you to set your heart on this promise?

Getting How It Fits into the Big Picture

8. In the Looking Forward portion of the teaching chapter, we read that God's original intention was for Adam to be fruitful and multiply and expand the borders of Eden so that eventually the entire earth would be filled with the glory and beauty and abundance of the Lord that they enjoyed in Eden. How did the second Adam succeed where the first Adam failed? And how does this help us to understand God's purposes for creation and redemption, which make up the story of the Bible?

Week 10

Malachi

Malachi

1. Malachi was a prophet in Israel after the return from exile in Babylon. He prophesied around the time of the events that take place in the book of Nehemiah. In the first verse of Malachi we learn that what follows is an oracle of the word of the Lord to Israel by Malachi. *Oracle* could also be translated as "burden." Considering the messages we have read throughout this study that were given through the prophets and the message Malachi is about to deliver, why do you think it could be accurately described as a "burden"?

2. The book of Malachi is made up primarily of a series of disputations between God and the collective voice of his people as evidenced in their attitudes toward him. In each disputation God deals with a particular problem. Read through the following passages in Malachi and summarize the problem God is confronting in each.

1:2–5

1:6–14

2:1–9

2:10–16

2:17

3:6–12

3:13–15

3. Malachi uses the title "LORD of hosts" for God twenty-four times in this short book. To call God "LORD of hosts" recognizes him as having a large contingent of heavenly beings at his command as well as authority throughout the earth. Considering the political situation of the people in Malachi's day, as well as the people's attitudes and actions toward God, why might Malachi have wanted to emphasize this aspect of who God is?

4. In Malachi 3:1–4 God provides an answer to the people's question, "Where is the God of justice?" (Mal. 2:17). See if you can put God's response into your own words.

5. In Malachi 3:16–18 it appears we are reading the record of the remnant who responded to Malachi's message. What does it reveal about what can be expected by those who fear the Lord?

6. In Malachi 4:1–2 the prophet describes what will happen in the Day of the Lord, and there is clearly a difference between what evildoers can expect and what those who fear the Lord can expect. What is it?

7. In Malachi 4:5–6 the prophet tells us more about the messenger he mentioned in 3:1, calling him "Elijah the prophet." What do these verses tell us about what he will be like, when he will come, and what will be the hallmark of his ministry?

8. After God spoke through the prophet Malachi, he did not speak directly to his people again for four hundred years. Then, finally, an angel appeared and spoke to a priest named Zechariah, who was burning incense in the temple. What was the angel's message, according to Luke 1:13–17?

9. In Matthew 11:7–15 what insight does Jesus provide about Malachi 3:1?

10. In John 1:31–34 what testimony does John the Baptist provide about the aim of his ministry?

Teaching Chapter

The Problem and the Promise

The story of the Bible is like a great drama presented in two acts. In our study of the prophets we come with the book of Malachi to the end of act 1. Before act 2 begins, with the Gospel of Matthew, there is a four-hundred-year intermission. The curtain opened in act 1 to the scene of a breathtaking garden paradise where Adam and Eve enjoyed a perfect relationship with each other and with the God who made them. God showered them with everything good and gave them clear instruction that would protect them from the evil that would destroy the goodness they enjoyed. But a serpent slithered into the garden and lied to Eve, telling her that God was withholding something good from them. So before the story had barely begun, everything about this first scene changed. They went from enjoying rich relationship with God and each other to being alienated from God and suspicious of each other. The aspects of their lives that were intended to provide their greatest pleasure began to bring pain and frustration. They were ejected from the place where they had known only God's blessing and sent out to live in the wilderness of a world under a curse. At the end of the first scene of act 1, we see Adam and Eve on the edge of the stage, looking back wistfully at the garden, which is now guarded by cherubim wielding flaming swords so that they can't get back in.

This scene presents to us the great problem the rest of the Bible seeks to remedy: God's people are now alienated from him, and from each other, existing for a limited lifetime in an environment in which the curse of sin has infiltrated and infected everything and everyone so that nothing works as it was supposed to, and no one is who they were meant to be. Intimate fellowship has given way to alienation. Life now ends in death. Pure worship of God has been infected with suspicion of God. Enjoying God's blessing in his world has become overshadowed by the effects of God's curse on the world.

But right here at the beginning of act 1, there is also a promise. God is going to deal with this profound problem. One day a child will be born to a daughter of Eve, and this Promised One will put an end to all the misery introduced into the world, and the way he will do it is by crushing the head of the ancient Serpent, who is Satan.

So from the first baby born to Eve, they began to wonder if this child was the Promised One. People began to call on the name of the Lord, asking him to send this promised child, who would deal with the problem of sin and alienation. And God began working out his plan to do just that. God called one man to himself—Abraham—and told him that he would be the father of a great people through whom this Promised One would come, the one through whom all the nations of the earth would be blessed. Abraham's family grew into a great nation, which became enslaved in Egypt. So God sent a deliverer, Moses, who led them out of slavery and gave them God's law. They made their home in the Promised Land, where God gave them a good king and promised that one of the king's descendants would sit on his throne and rule forever. But the reality was that all the kings who followed this king, David, and sat on his throne proved to be a disappointment. Rather than ruling in righteousness, they led the people into idolatry. Rather than impressing upon them the joy of loving and living in the ways of God, these kings led them in despising the ways of God and defiling the temple of God. Sadly, just as God's first son, Adam, had failed to obey in the garden and was exiled from Eden, so this son, the nation of Israel, failed to obey and was exiled from the Promised Land. But not forever.

As we come to the end of act 1, in the book of Malachi, a small remnant of those who were exiled are now back at home in Jerusalem. These are people who grew up reading Isaiah and Jeremiah and Ezekiel's prophecies of restoration. Some of these people came back to the land under the leadership of Zerubbabel and rebuilt the temple. But the temple is not nearly as magnificent as it was in the days of Solomon and nowhere near the description of the glorious new temple that Ezekiel described. They are planting crops, but nowhere near the abundant replanting that Ezekiel wrote about. The dirt is as hard and resistant as it was when Adam and Eve began working out in the wilderness. Under Nehemiah's leadership they have rebuilt the walls of Jerusalem, yet they are still under the thumb of Persia, with a puppet king on the throne who is not a descendant of David, let alone the great king the prophets promised. Jeremiah and Ezekiel prophesied that the people would be given new hearts to love and obey the Lord, but the truth is they have really grown weary of the Lord. They are going through the motions of bringing sacrifices and offerings to the rebuilt temple, but they're not bringing their best. With so many promises not yet fulfilled, they are wondering if a relationship with God is worth all the effort.

And some of us know what that is like. We've fed on the promises of God throughout the Scriptures and we've taken them to heart. We've believed and we've waited, and the reality of day-to-day life is nothing like what we understood was being held out to us. It makes us wonder if all this following and believing and waiting is really worth it—if God is really worthy of all he requires of us.

Malachi Demonstrates the Problem

And so the Word of the Lord comes to his prophet, Malachi, to be given to a cynical, apathetic, disappointed people. And by what the Lord has to say, it is clear that there are problems, and, really, they are the same problems God's people have dealt with ever since Adam and Eve were exiled from Eden.

There's a problem with their receptivity to God's love. We hear a broken heart speaking in the first words that God wants Malachi to say to his people on his behalf:

> "I have loved you," says the LORD. But you say, "How have you loved us?"
> (Mal. 1:2)

By their skeptical response to God's laying his heart out on the table, we see how the relationship has devolved. They want to define how God should demonstrate his love for them. They want everything that Ezekiel and so many of the other prophets wrote about—the future of restoration and wholeness and blessing—to be their reality in the here and now. That's the only way they will believe that God loves them. But God has a very different way of defending his claims of love. In fact, his answer actually seems like a problem to many of us, just cause for questioning his love. So we need to allow God, who is love, to show us what his love looks like.

> "Is not Esau Jacob's brother?" declares the LORD. "Yet I have loved Jacob but Esau I have hated." (Mal. 1:2–3)

We might expect God to answer this question about how he has loved them with something like, "I brought you out of slavery. I provided for you in the wilderness. I gave you a vast land and a good king. I brought you back from exile. I forgave you. I cared for you. I've been patient with you. I've provided for you." All of that is true. But God's response is quite different. He says, *I have loved you by choosing you to be mine when you had done nothing to deserve my choosing.* God's love, which was set on Jacob and his descendants, isn't about personality or performance or likability but only about his sovereign, electing choice. God tells his people through Malachi in the verses that follow, *I am loving you by giving you all the benefits of belonging to me and not to the world. And I will love you by bringing to destruction all those who show their hate for me by their cruelty toward you.*

Secondly, there's a problem with a lack of respect in how sacrifices are being offered. Reverence and respect are the appropriate responses toward a God who has lovingly chosen them, but God's people apparently have so little regard for God that they are actually dishonoring him, even as they go through the motions of offering sacrifices at the temple. So God asks:

> When you offer blind animals in sacrifice, is that not evil? And when you offer those that are lame or sick, is that not evil? (Mal. 1:8)

They know what is required by the law of Moses. They are supposed to bring unblemished animals, the first and best of their har-
vests, but they are instead picking out animals that are no good to
them anyway and taking them to the temple. And we recognize that
this is an age-old problem dating back to when Abel pleased God by
bringing the firstborn and best of his flock, while Cain brought a token
bit of grain. As we think about it, we realize it isn't really a problem
with grain or animals but a problem of the heart—hearts that have so
little respect for God that they want to give the minimum rather than to
truly honor God with their first and best. Malachi points out that they
would never present such second-rate gifts to their governor, someone
in the secular realm they want to honor, yet they have no qualms about
bringing second-rate offerings to their great King. And what is their
response to this challenge? They say, "What a weariness this is" (1:13).
You can almost hear them sighing and rolling their eyes like adoles-
cents. They are clearly bored with God and don't want to be bothered
with his commands.

They think that because they've put a tip on the table, they have
been true to him. Throughout this whole first act, this has been a
symptom of a people who think God will be content with something
less than love. The great commandment was and is, "You shall love the
LORD your God with all your heart and with all your soul and with all
your might" (Deut. 6:5). Nothing else and nothing less will satisfy God.
But here are people who have been surrounded by God's love and have
received his grace for centuries, yet their hearts are so cold that they
can't see that they are insulting God by their pathetic presentations at
his table.

It causes us to think, doesn't it, about what we are saying to God
when we are consistently late to worship, when we're bored with
him while we're there, getting credit for attendance even though our
thoughts are elsewhere? What kind of insult is it to God when we show
up in order to be seen at worship, yet our hearts are never broken by
our sin and our spirits never soar over his goodness?

Third, there's a problem with the instruction given by the priests. God
speaks through Malachi to his priests who have fallen so far from all

that God intended his priests to be and do when he entrusted the tribe
of Levi to this task:

> For the lips of a priest should guard knowledge, and people should seek
> instruction from his mouth, for he is the messenger of the LORD of hosts.
> But you have turned aside from the way. You have caused many to stum-
> ble by your instruction. You have corrupted the covenant of Levi, says the
> LORD of hosts. (Mal. 2:7–8)

The priests, who are supposed to teach the Word of God, are not listening to the Word themselves (2:1). They simply have no real burden,
no real heart, to give glory to God but are consumed with lesser things,
perhaps things that seem more practical, more popular, and more profitable (2:2, 9). Perhaps they started out in ministry wanting to be all
God intended them to be, but somewhere along the way, Malachi says,
they have "turned aside from the way" (2:8).

How many people in our day have given up on God because of the
hypocrisy, worldliness, greed, and utter moral bankruptcy of those
who have been entrusted with leadership in the church? The prophet
Malachi has a message for all who have turned away from the church
because a leader has "turned aside from the way," which is that God
hates priestly hypocrisy far more than you do.

Fourth, there's a problem with their rejection of their wives. When God
made Adam and Eve one flesh, he filled their union not only with pleasure but also with purpose. He told them to "be fruitful and multiply
and fill the earth" (Gen. 1:28). They were to populate the earth with
descendants who would reflect the image of God, living in glad obedience to God. But there was a problem then, which was quickly made
evident when Cain killed Abel, and there continues to be a problem in
Malachi's day.

> For Judah has profaned the sanctuary of the LORD, which he loves, and
> has married the daughter of a foreign god. (Mal. 2:11)

The problem with this intermarriage with women from other countries was not racial; it was religious. Throughout the Old Testament we

see that there are those outside the family of Israel—women such as Rahab and Ruth who take hold by faith of Israel's God and go from foreigner to family. The problem in Malachi's day was that men of Israel, who had been set apart to God and were to raise children who would love and obey God, were marrying women who served other gods and had no ability, let alone desire, to train up children to love Yahweh alone.

Not only are men of Judah marrying women who worship false gods; they are abandoning their Israelite wives, whom they covenanted before God to be united to for life, to marry these women:

> The LORD was witness between you and the wife of your youth, to whom you have been faithless, though she is your companion and your wife by covenant. Did he not make them one, with a portion of the Spirit in their union? And what was the one God seeking? Godly offspring. (Mal. 2:14–15)

These marriages were being forsaken, perhaps for sexual attraction toward another, but more likely for the political or financial advantage gained by marriage to a non-Israelite. Fulfilling their own desires, they ignored the Lord's desire that he would have a holy people for himself who are wholly devoted to him. These divorces, in which wives from within the covenant community were being sent away to make room for women who worshiped foreign gods, meant that the men of Israel were completely abdicating their responsibility to raise children "in the discipline and instruction of the Lord" (Eph. 6:4).

Fifth, there's a problem with their responsibilities as God's stewards. Ever since God brought his people into the Promised Land, he made it clear that the land was still his, and they were tenants on it (Lev. 25:23). Likewise, everything he blessed them with was really his and was entrusted to them to employ for his kingdom purposes. But they were like us. We have a tendency to hoard and hide what God entrusts to us, acting as if it really belongs to us to do with as we please. To those entrusted as stewards of all that really belongs to him, God says:

> Return to me, and I will return to you, says the LORD of hosts. But you say, "How shall we return?" Will man rob God? Yet you are robbing me.

But you say, "How have we robbed you?" In your tithes and contributions.
(Mal. 3:7–8)

Really, this is about much more than a reluctance to tithe. Their
unwillingness to give freely and generously to God's service was symp-
tomatic of a deeper issue that communicated a far greater insult. They
saw God and his ministry to them through his temple as unworthy
of their investment. There was something more important to them
than giving God his due, and that was getting and keeping what they
desired. Malachi invited God's people to demonstrate their trust in
God and love for God by giving to him what really belonged to him in
the first place, promising that as they returned in faithfulness to their
covenantal obligations, he would be faithful to them in his covenant
promises to bless them (Mal. 3:7).

Our giving or lack thereof is a window into how we see really see
God and how we see ourselves. If we see God as a gracious giver, and
if we see ourselves as stewards of all he has entrusted to us, we will be
glad givers, confident that he will always provide what we need. But if
we see him as unworthy and ourselves as the ones who have generated
our wealth, it will be obvious in our reluctant giving.

Sixth, there's a problem with their rhetoric regarding God's justice.
Their lips should be telling of his goodness, but they don't see him as
good. They should be celebrating his justice, but they think they're getting a raw deal. They should be bragging about the benefits of belonging to God, but they claim that serving him is useless:

> Your words have been hard against me, says the LORD. But you say, "How
> have we spoken against you?" You have said, "It is vain to serve God. What
> is the profit of our keeping his charge or of walking as in mourning before
> the LORD of hosts? And now we call the arrogant blessed. Evildoers not
> only prosper but they put God to the test and they escape." (Mal. 3:13–15)

We've heard before this complaint about evildoers prospering, especially in the Psalms. But the people in Malachi's day are not taking their
complaint to God and asking him to shed light on it. They are not talking to him at all. They have come to the settled conclusion that God is

not worth the effort, that there is no benefit to belonging to him, no blessing in serving him. As far as they can see, people who have no use for God are doing just fine, perhaps even better than they are.

Malachi Declares the Promise

Malachi has stated the all-too-familiar problems of the people of his day clearly. But along with detailing the problem, Malachi, like so many prophets before him, also declares God's promise. And, like the prophets before him, the promise centers on a person.

First, there's the promise of a refiner. Malachi, whose name means "my messenger," presents hope to a people who cannot seem to overcome the problems that have plagued them for centuries by telling them about two messengers who are going to come:

> Behold, I send my messenger, and he will prepare the way before me. And the Lord whom you seek will suddenly come to his temple; and the messenger of the covenant in whom you delight, behold, he is coming, says the LORD of hosts. (Mal. 3:1)

One messenger will prepare the way for the Lord to come. And then the "messenger of the covenant" who is at the same time both a messenger for the Lord and the Lord himself, will "suddenly come to his temple." All Ezekiel's prophecies about the glory of God returning to his temple are going to become reality. This is what they have longed for and hoped for. But it may also be more than they have bargained for:

> Who can endure the day of his coming, and who can stand when he appears? For he is like a refiner's fire and like fullers' soap. He will sit as a refiner and purifier of silver, and he will purify the sons of Levi and refine them like gold and silver, and they will bring offerings in righteousness to the LORD. Then the offering of Judah and Jerusalem will be pleasing to the LORD as in the days of old and as in former years. (Mal. 3:2–4)

The Lord's coming to his temple is not automatically good news for the people of Malachi's day, whether they realize it or not, because God cannot tolerate sin. However, the good news in Malachi's message is that when the messenger of the covenant comes, he is going to deal with their sin. He is going to do a work of refining God's people like a silversmith refines silver—plunging it into the fire and holding it there while everything impure is melted away so that when it comes out of the fire, it is pure and radiant. He is going to come like a launderer, washing away their dirty little habits and unwholesome ways of thinking and feeling. He's going to cleanse and purify them so they will have nothing to fear when they stand in God's presence.

These people have claimed that they want God to be just, but that is not really what they want. What they need instead of justice is mercy and grace. And Malachi tells them that when God comes in the person of his Son, he will not immediately judge sin even though that's what they deserve. He's coming the first time to do a gracious work of redemption, to purify those he has loved and chosen. How will he purify them? By taking their impurity upon himself and beginning an ongoing work of purification in them by his Spirit. Only after his work of gracious redemption has its full effect will he return in judgment.

Second, there's the promise of a book of remembrance. When the messenger comes, he will have with him a book:

> Then those who feared the LORD spoke with one another. The LORD paid attention and heard them, and a book of remembrance was written before him of those who feared the LORD and esteemed his name. "They shall be mine, says the LORD of hosts, in the day when I make up my treasured possession, and I will spare them as a man spares his son who serves him. Then once more you shall see the distinction between the righteous and the wicked, between one who serves God and one who does not serve him. (Mal. 3:16–18)

This is the book that is mentioned throughout Scripture (Ex. 32:32; Rev. 20:12–15), the book that has the list of names of those who belong to God, a list of all of those who deserve to be destroyed by fire but have instead been refined and purified by it, a list of the names of people who have esteemed the name of the Lord more than life itself. For all those whose rhetoric has been filled with accusations that they have served God in vain, since the wicked seem to be enjoying as much or more blessing than they have, here is the fuller picture beyond what they can see in the here and now. There *will be* a distinction between those who cry out for mercy and receive the righteousness of Christ and those who wickedly ignore or reject him. Clearly, we do not serve the Lord in vain, even if we never experience in this lifetime everything he has promised. The day will come when we will see the full benefit of belonging to him.

The third promise Malachi presents is the coming of the sun of righteousness. As he gives God's people this promise, the very different futures for those who fear the Lord and those who do not come into even clearer focus:

> For behold, the day is coming, burning like an oven, when all the arrogant and all evildoers will be stubble. The day that is coming shall set them ablaze, says the LORD of hosts, so that it will leave them neither root nor branch. But for you who fear my name, the sun of righteousness shall rise with healing in its wings. You shall go out leaping like calves from the stall. (Mal. 4:1–2)

Fire burns and destroys, but it also has the power to cleanse and heal. Malachi looks into the future and sees a burning fire that consumes those who have rejected and rebelled against God. But that same fire, a fire that is like the sun, beams down its rays on those who fear God and does a work of healing so that there is new life and energy for a future to be enjoyed in his presence.

That is the message of Malachi. If we were sitting in the theatre watching act 1 of the story of the Bible, when we got to the end Malachi we would be encouraged by these promises. But perhaps we would also think that we've heard them before. Perhaps we would wonder when and how all these promises are going to be fulfilled. We could not help but be struck by the reality that these people are still plagued with the same problems they had back at the beginning of the Bible's story.

These people in the story have been brought out of slavery; they've been given God's law to live by so that they will be different from all of the peoples around them. They were given a good king, and the cloud of God's presence came down and filled their temple. Yet the main problems of alienation from God and the effects of the curse show no signs of being addressed. They are as far away from God here at the end of act 1 as they were when Adam and Eve got tossed out of the garden. In fact, their hearts have only gotten harder. And the curse that has hung over them is still there. There can be no happy ending unless that problem is solved. The story that began in Genesis with God's blessing ends here in Malachi with God threatening to "come and strike the land with a curse" (Mal. 4:6 NLT). That is actually the last word of Malachi in several translations, the last word of the Old Testament: curse.

As we take our seat back in the theater for the second act, we wonder what it is going to take to change this fundamental hardness in the human heart, what it is going to take for this curse to be gone for good, since clearly all of their religious activity hasn't solved the problem.

Jesus Deals with the Problem

Then the curtain rises, and before us is a scene set in a stable where a new baby is lying in a feed trough wrapped in rags. And we begin to wonder, *Could it be that this little baby will deal with the problem?* Over the course of act 2 we discover that he is the Promised One who has come to deal with the central problem of the Old Testament—human sin, and all of its effects still evident in Malachi's day.

~ Jesus will deal with their doubts about God's love by demonstrating his love "in that while we were still sinners, Christ died for us" (Rom. 5:8). When we ask God, "How have you loved us?" we hear, "He chose us in him before the foundation of the world, that we should be holy and blameless before him. In love he predestined us for adoption as sons through Jesus Christ" (Eph. 1:4–5).

~ Jesus will deal with the lack of respect his people show to God through their sickly sacrifices by offering himself as the once-for-all sacrifice, "a fragrant offering, a sacrifice acceptable and pleasing to God" (Phil. 4:18).

~ Jesus will deal with the problem of priests who have despised his name and corrupted his covenant by becoming the Great High Priest, who will instruct his people with a sense of authority his people have never heard before and integrity they've never seen before (Matt. 7:28–29).

～ Jesus will deal with the problem of faithless husbands as he loves the wife of his youth, his bride, the church, and will not be faithless toward her. In fact, he will credit his own faithfulness to all who are joined to him by faith (Eph. 5:25–27).

～ Jesus will not withhold anything that God requires but will fulfill the righteous requirement of the law on our behalf (Rom. 8:3–4).

～ Jesus will deal with his people's questions about God's justice by seeing to it that no evil will go unpunished. He will experience on the cross the punishment his people deserve. And when he comes again, he will punish all the evil that was not dealt with there.

～ Jesus will deal with the problem of the curse by taking it upon himself, "becoming a curse for us" (Gal. 3:13).

Jesus Delivers on the Promise

In act 2 we see Jesus solve the problems that could never get solved throughout the whole of the Old Testament: sin and the curse. Likewise, we also see him deliver on the promise of the Old Testament, including the promise found in Malachi.

We see the Lord come suddenly to his temple as Jesus steps onto the stage of human history, teaching and healing in the temple, and cleansing the temple in his zeal for his Father's house. We see him come as a refiner who is even now at work in us by his Spirit burning away the impurities of our pride and apathy and unbelief. He is removing what is unfit and displeasing, transforming the ordinary ore of our lives into a shining treasure that reflects his image. The sun of righteousness dawned on the people of Jesus's day when he came as the light of the world. He shines down on us even now as he brings healing to the wounds and scars sin has left on our souls.

And he will come suddenly a second time. He will have his book of remembrance in his hands, which contains the names of all who fear his name, shown by the way they run to him in repentance and walk with him in obedience. For them, the fiery nature of his second coming will be that of a fire that heals as it burns away every lingering evidence of decay. The sun of righteousness will yet rise on the dawn of a new day and a new creation.

At the end of act 2 will come "the great and awesome day of the LORD" (Mal. 4:5). That's when we will finally experience the happy ending we all long for in this grand story. The problem of human sin and its curse will be gone for good. The promise will have been fulfilled as the Promised One will have come to stay. The Lamb of God will have taken away the sin of the world. The Son of David will be seated on David's throne. The Wisdom of God will have overcome the foolishness of the world. The Word of the Lord who came will come again. This time, instead of coming to die for us, he will come to live with us. The curtain will open to a grand new story in which every scene will be better than the one before.[16]

Looking Forward

Who Can Stand When He Appears?

The people of Malachi's day were saying, "Everyone who does evil is good in the sight of the LORD, and he delights in them" (Mal. 2:17). As far as they could see, God was actually taking delight in evil people, and they wanted God to show up and punish them instead. They were asking, "Where is the God of justice?" (v. 17).

Malachi answered that God was going to show up but that they might get more than they bargained for at his coming. They think all the evil people are "out there." They've been too arrogant, too obtuse, to see the evil inside themselves that rightly deserves the justice of God. So Malachi asks them a question that should make them think again about their desire for the God of justice to show up:

> But who can endure the day of his coming, and who can stand when he appears? (Mal. 3:2)

This question should make us think deeply as well. Who can endure the day of his coming? What makes me think that I will somehow escape his judgment? On what basis do I think I will be able to stand before him when he appears and not be immediately cast from his holy presence?

Paul expressed confidence in regard to this day when he asked, "If God is for us, who can be against us?" (Rom. 8:31). In sending the Promised One to deal with the problem of sin, God showed us that he is for us, not against us. Because he has loved us with his sovereign, electing love, though we have done evil, we do not have to fear standing before him. In his first coming, Jesus did what was necessary to make it possible for sinners to stand before God when he comes again. In fact, because of the sufficiency of his payment for our sin and because of the security found in being united to him, nothing and no one can effectively stand against us.

> Who shall bring any charge against God's elect? It is God who justifies. Who is to condemn? Christ Jesus is the one who died—more than that, who was raised—who is at the right hand of God, who indeed is interceding for us. (Rom. 8:33–34)

On that day when he appears and we stand before God, the refiner's work will be complete so that we will reflect God's glory to him. He will find our name there in his book of remembrance. The sun of righteousness will have healed us and made us beautiful and pleasing in God's sight. On our own, we could never dare to stand before the withering judgment of the holy God. But Jesus has satisfied God's justice, he has purified and healed us, and he will be there standing with us. So when we hear Malachi ask, "Who can stand when he appears?" we can answer, "I can. I will be able to stand and face him. But it won't be because of anything I am or anything I've done. I will be able to stand on that day only because Jesus is mine and I am his."

Discussion Guide
Malachi

Getting the Discussion Going

1. Imagine yourself as one of the people living in Jerusalem a number of years after the exile in Babylon. You've read all the promises the prophets have made, and yet life is hard. Your country is still ruled by a foreign power, the economy is not good, and, honestly, the rebuilt temple and the city are a bit of a disappointment. What would you be thinking and feeling about God and his promises and plans for your people?

Getting to the Heart of It

2. Isn't it interesting that God begins this final message to his people before four hundred years of prophetic silence by saying, "I have loved you." But perhaps even more interesting is how he defines that love. How has he loved them, according to Malachi 1:2–5?

3. The priests of Malachi's day were allowing people to bring sickly, injured animals to offer as sacrifices. What did that kind of offering reveal about their hearts?

4. What are some ways we dishonor God in how we approach him in worship and in what we give to him? What does this reveal about our hearts?

5. When we hear the Lord's indictment regarding marriages to foreign wives and divorcing covenant wives, we jump quickly to making it about marriage and divorce in our day. And certainly there are implications here about marriage to unbelievers and about divorce. But as we first try to think through what God was getting at in their day and situation, why was God displeased?

6. What is Malachi's answer to the people's desire that God come and execute justice?

Getting Personal

7. Malachi promises that Jesus is going to come to refine and cleanse and heal. How has the Lord worked in your heart and your life to refine and cleanse and heal during the course of this study?

Getting How It Fits into the Big Picture

8. One of the reasons the people of Malachi's day were so disillusioned with God was that they had read all the promises of the prophets and they didn't see them becoming reality. What would you want to tell them, if you could, from your perspective of having the whole of the Old and New Testaments?

Bibliography

Books and Articles

Beale, G. K. *The Temple and the Church's Mission: A Biblical Theology of the Dwelling Place of God.* Downers Grove, IL: InterVarsity, 2004.

Begg, Alistair, and Sinclair Ferguson. *Name Above All Names.* Wheaton, IL: Crossway, 2013.

Beynon, Nigel. "The Adultery." http://beginningwithmoses.org/bt-briefings/170/the-adultery, accessed June 24, 2011.

Blackham, Paul. *Daniel.* Book by Book Study Guide. London: Biblical Frameworks, 2009.

———. *Isaiah.* Book by Book Study Guide. London: Biblical Frameworks, 2011.

———. *Jonah.* Book by Book Study Guide. Carlisle, UK: Authentic Media, 2003.

Boice, James Montgomery. *The Minor Prophets.* Vol. 1, *Hosea–Jonah.* Grand Rapids, MI: Baker, 1983.

Clowney, Edmund. "The Final Temple." *Westminster Theological Journal* 35 (1973): 156–91.

Dever, Mark. *The Message of the Old Testament: Promises Made.* Wheaton, IL: Crossway, 2006.

Duguid, Iain M. *Daniel.* Reformed Expository Commentary. Phillipsburg, NJ: P&R, 2008.

———. *Ezekiel.* NIV Application Commentary. Grand Rapids, MI: Zondervan, 1999.

———. *Haggai, Zechariah, Malachi.* EP Study Commentary. Carlisle, PA: EP Books, 2010.

Ferguson, Sinclair B. *Daniel.* The Preacher's Commentary. Nashville, TN: Thomas Nelson, 1988.

———. *The Holy Spirit: Contours of Christian Theology.* Downers Grove, IL: IVP Academic, 1997.

———. *Man Overboard!: The Story of Jonah.* Carlisle, PA: Banner of Truth, 1981.

Guthrie, Nancy. *The One Year Book of Discovering Jesus in the Old Testament.* Carol Stream, IL: Tyndale, 2010.

Kidner, Derek. *The Message of Hosea.* The Bible Speaks Today. Downers Grove, IL: InterVarsity, 1981.

Murray, David. *Jesus on Every Page.* Nashville, TN: Thomas Nelson, 2013.

Nelson, Jared. "Two Complaints or The Gospel According to Habakkuk." http://
    deadtheologians.blogspot.com/2009/10/sermon-text-habakkuks-two
    -complaints.html.

Ortlund, Raymond C., Jr. *Isaiah: God Saves Sinners*. Preaching the Word. Wheaton,
    IL: Crossway, 2005.

Phillips, Richard D. *Jonah and Micah*. Reformed Expository Commentary. Phillips-
    burg, NJ: P&R, 2010.

Roberts, Vaughan. *God's Big Picture: Tracing the Storyline of the Bible*. Downers
    Grove, IL: InterVarsity, 2002.

Robertson, O. Palmer. *Christ of the Prophets*. Abridged edition. Phillipsburg, NJ:
    P&R, 2008.

Ryken, Philip Graham. *Jeremiah and Lamentations: From Sorrow to Hope*. Preaching
    the Word. Wheaton, IL: Crossway, 2001.

Schwab, George. *Hope in the Midst of a Hostile World: The Gospel according to Daniel*.
    Phillipsburg, NJ: P&R, 2006.

Selvaggio, Anthony. *The Prophets Speak of Him: Encountering Jesus in the Minor
    Prophets*. Webster, NY: Evangelical Press, 2006.

Audio

Ash, Christopher. "Daniel." Sermon series. All Saints, Little Shelford, England, 1998.

———. "The Sign of Jonah." Sermon. All Saints, Little Shelford, England, October
    21, 2001.

Bewes, Richard. "The Prophet of Restitution: Micah." Sermon. All Souls Langham
    Place, London, July 10, 1988.

———. "Walking on Air." Sermon. All Souls Langham Place, London, June 14, 1998.

———. "A Young Heart." Sermon. All Souls Langham Place, London, November 15,
    2000.

Beynon, Nigel. "Hosea: A Love Story." Sermon series. St. Helen's Bishopsgate,
    London, February 2000.

Blackham, Paul. "Jonah: To a City That Repented." Sermon. All Souls Langham
    Place, London, January 17, 1999.

———. "Meet the Servant." Sermon. All Souls Langham Place, London, March 22,
    1998.

———. "Will God Win?" Sermon. All Souls Langham Place, London, May 31, 1998.

———. "Tried by Fire." Sermon. All Souls Langham Place, London, November 12,
    2003.

———. "What God Requires." Sermon. All Souls Langham Place, London, August 27,
    2006.

———. "Will God Win?" Sermon. All Souls Langham Place, London, May 31, 1998.

Carson, D. A. "Jeremiah 30–31." Sermon. Castlewellan, Northern Ireland, December
    13, 2007.

———. "Jesus the Temple of God." Sermon. Chesterton House, Cornell University, Ithaca, NY, February 2002.

DeYoung, Kevin. "Revelation 22:1–5." Sermon. University Reformed Church, Lansing, MI, August 5, 2007.

Duguid, Iain. "Jonah." Sermon series. Christ Presbyterian Church, Grove City, PA, July 2010.

Goligher, Liam. "Ezekiel." Sermon series. Tenth Presbyterian Church, Philadelphia, 2012.

———. "The Final Temple." Sermon. Duke Street Church, London, January 31, 2010.

———. "The Gospel according to Isaiah." Sermon series. Duke Street Church, London, 2007.

———. "The New Covenant." Sermon. Duke Street Church, London, November 14, 2010.

Helm, David. "Questions for God." Sermon series on Habakkuk. Holy Trinity Church, Chicago, IL, 2012.

Jackman, David. "Learning." Sermon. St. Helen's Bishopsgate, London, November 17, 1996.

———. "Waiting for Fulfillment: Jeremiah to Malachi." The Christian Institute, Newcastle, UK, September 17, 1994.

Jackson, Arthur. "The Bible: Isaiah to Malachi." Lecture. Holy Trinity Church, Chicago, February 28, 2010.

Jensen, Peter. "Understanding the Prophets." Lecture. Katoomba Houseparty, Katoomba, New South Wales, Australia, 1998.

Keller, Timothy J. "The True Bridegroom." Sermon. Redeemer Presbyterian Church, New York, December 2, 2007.

Kelly, Scott. "The Gospel in Micah." Sermon series. Christ Church, Lafayette, CO, 2012.

Messner, Aaron. "Micah: The Man and His Times." Sermon series. Tenth Presbyterian Church, Philadelphia, 2007.

Olyott, Stuart. "Intro to Ezekiel, Why a Man Who Has God's Word Must Speak It, and Why We Must Hear It." Sermon. Belvidere Road Church, Liverpool, UK, 1974.

———. "An Introduction to Isaiah and the Book." Sermon. Belvidere Road Church, Liverpool, UK, 1974.

———. "Promised Land to Exile." Sermon series. Belvidere Road Church, Liverpool, UK, 1979.

Piper, John. "Call Me Husband, Not Baal." Sermon. Bethlehem Baptist Church, Minneapolis, December 26, 1982.

Pratt, Richard. "He Gave Us Prophets." Lecture series. Third Millennium Ministries, 2007.

Roberts, Vaughan. "Hosea." Sermon series. Crieff Fellowship, Scotland, January 2007.

Smith, Colin. "Close Encounters with the Living God." Sermon series on Micah. The Orchard Evangelical Free Church, Arlington Heights, IL, 2005.

———. "How to Avoid a God-Centered Life." Sermon series on Jonah. The Orchard Evangelical Free Church, Arlington Heights, IL, 2009.

———. "Restore My Soul: Nine Heart-Cries for Revival." Sermon Series on Isaiah. The Orchard Evangelical Free Church, Arlington Heights, IL, 2008.

———. "Unlocking the Bible in Daniel and the Minor Prophets." Sermon series. The Orchard Evangelical Free Church, Arlington Heights, IL, 2000.

———. "Unlocking the Bible in Isaiah and Jeremiah." Sermon series. The Orchard Evangelical Free Church, Arlington Heights, IL, 2000.

———. "Unlocking the Bible in Lamentations and Ezekiel." Sermon series. The Orchard Evangelical Free Church, Arlington Heights, IL, 2000.

Tice, Rico. "Our God Is Marching On." Sermon. All Souls Langham Place, London, June 7, 1998.

———. "The Suffering Servant." Sermon. All Souls Langham Place, London, April 5, 1998.

Woodhouse, John. "Facing the Real King." Sermon. Christ Church, St. Ives, Australia. November 13, 1994.

———. "Hopeless Hopes." Sermon series on Ezekiel. Christ Church, St. Ives, Australia. 1991.

———. "Jonah." Sermon series. Christ Church, St. Ives, Australia. 1997.

———. "Prophecy: Isaiah to Malachi." Sermon. Christ Church, St. Ives, Australia. March 12, 1997.

———. "Who Really Rules." Sermon series on Daniel. Christ Church, St. Ives, Australia. 1991.

Wright, Christopher. "God Arrives in Babylon." Sermon. All Souls Langham Place, London, June 8, 2005.

———. "The Suffering Servant." Sermon. All Souls Langham Place, London, April 14, 2006.

Notes

1 O. Palmer Robertson, *The Christ of the Prophets*, abridged ed. (Phillipsburg, NJ: P&R, 2008), 117.

2 Richard Pratt, "He Gave Us Prophets," lecture series, Third Millennium Ministries, 2007, http://thirdmill.org/seminary/course.asp/vs/HGP.

3 A prayer Colin Smith repeatedly commends in his helpful sermon series on Jonah, "How to Avoid a God-Centered Life," the Orchard Evangelical Free Church, Arlington Heights, IL, 2009.

4 Smith, "How to Avoid a God-Centered Life."

5 James Rowe, "Love Lifted Me," 1912.

6 Adapted from Nigel Benyon, "Hosea: A Love Story," sermon series, February 2000, St. Helens Bishopsgate, London.

7 Opening narration, *Law & Order* television series, producer Dick Wolf.

8 Friedrich Nietzche, *Beyond Good and Evil*, 1886.

9 Alec Motyer, *Isaiah by the Day* (Ross-shire, UK: Christian Focus, 2011), 75.

10 This recognition of the three viewpoints of the five stanzas of the hymn of Isaiah 52:13–53:12 comes from Rico Tice's sermon, "The Suffering Servant," April 5, 1998, All Souls Langham Place, London.

11 Helen H. Lemmel, "Turn Your Eyes upon Jesus," 1922.

12 Colin Smith, "Heart," sermon, October 8, 2000, The Orchard Evangelical Free Church, Arlington Heights, IL.

13 Christopher Ash, "Daniel 1: Discretion and Valour," sermon, April 26, 1998, All Saints Little Shelford, Cambridge, UK.

14 Douglas Sean O'Donnell, *The Beginning and End of Wisdom: Preaching Christ from the First and Last Chapters of Proverbs, Ecclesiastes, and Job* (Crossway, Wheaton, IL, 2011), 67.

15 G. K. Beale repeatedly describes the new heaven and the new earth as a "garden-like city in the shape of a temple" in, *The Temple and the Church's Mission: A Biblical Theology of the Dwelling Place of God* (Downers Grove, IL: InterVarsity, 2004).

16 Adapted from C. S. Lewis, *The Last Battle* (New York: HarperCollins 1956), 183. He wrote: "They were beginning Chapter One of the Great Story which no one on earth has read: which goes on forever: in which every chapter is better than the one before."

For additional content, downloads,
and resources for leaders, please visit:

SeeingJesusInTheOldTestament.com

Also Available in the
Seeing Jesus in the Old Testament Series

The Promised One: *Seeing Jesus in Genesis*

The Lamb of God: *Seeing Jesus in Exodus, Leviticus, Numbers,
and Deuteronomy*

The Son of David: *Seeing Jesus in the Historical Books*

The Wisdom of God: *Seeing Jesus in the Psalms and Wisdom Books*

The Word of the Lord: *Seeing Jesus in the Prophets*

A companion DVD is also available for each study.

SeeingJesusInTheOldTestament.com